FOREVER YOUNG

FOREVER YOUNG

BO ROBERTS

Edited by Leigh R. Hendry
Back cover photo by Mike DuBose
Headshot by Jerry Atnip

gatekeeper press
Columbus, Ohio

FOREVER YOUNG

The Youngest as a World's Fair President, Editor,
Governor's Cabinet Leader, University Vice President

Published by Gatekeeper Press
2167 Stringtown Rd, Suite 109
Columbus, OH 43123-2989
www.GatekeeperPress.com

The editorial work for this book is entirely the product of the author. Gatekeeper Press did not participate in and is not responsible for any aspect of these elements.

ISBN (hardcover): 9781662927379
eISBN: 9781662927386

CONTENTS

*

INTRODUCTION

When I was contacted in 1960 by a national publication regarding my status as the youngest newspaper editor in the nation, I was totally surprised. At the time, I was editing two weekly newspapers. A representative of an industry trade publication, *Publisher's Auxiliary*, called to say that they were planning to do a brief feature story about me. According to their canvassing, they had determined that I, at the age of 23, was America's youngest newspaper editor. That's how I first became aware of this specific statistic.

The "youngest age ever" situation would develop several more times during the circuitous course of my career. At the age of 28, I became the youngest member of a governor's cabinet in the history of the state of Tennessee, and at 33, I became the youngest person to be appointed as a vice president at the University of Tennessee, Knoxville. In both of those cases, it was usually members of the media who brought the designation to my attention. A bit later in my career, at the age of 39, I was recognized as the youngest president of an international World's Fair in the history of expositions. Again, I didn't know this until someone called it to my attention.

And, that's how the "youngest ever" classification evolved.

In none of those instances was I seeking to be "the youngest" of anything. They occurred organically, and without premeditation on my part. Now, being a naturally competitive person, if there'd been a category for that achievement in the *Guinness Book of World Records,* I might have taken it more seriously. Little did I know that it would become a continuing thread throughout my professional life. As the years have gone on, it's been quite a while since I've had the distinction of being "the youngest" of anything. I don't expect that I will hold that title again, unless I become the youngest president of an octogenarian club, perhaps. When queried about my plans to retire recently, I said: "I'll stop when I don't enjoy it anymore. I don't allow chronology to define either how I feel or what I plan to do."

In attempting to write this book, I realized that I'd had a plethora of unique experiences. Because some of these have spanned pivotal national and international events, I wanted to convey, not a history of those times, but my personal reaction to those particular moments. Even though I was a small, tangential part of events in some cases, I wanted to capture how I felt and what these instances meant to me. They include a KKK cross being burned in my front yard, the assassination of Martin Luther King in Tennessee, the wild and crazy 1968 Democratic Convention, the cancellation of the U.S. participation in the 1980 Olympics, recruiting the People's Republic of China to its first ever World's Fair, and leading the reorganization of higher education in Tennessee. While I have been as historically accurate as possible, this is a compilation of my reactions and observations, not a chronicle of history.

As I continue to move along in life, I still hope to be a part of history. We are blessed to be on this earth and citizens of this country, which, flawed though it may be, remains the world's finest. I hope you'll enjoy both the journey and seeing the world as I've seen it. Longevity produces many experiences, and, if we're lucky, imparts a scintilla of wisdom. As you'll note, my path has been meandering, sometimes disjointed, occasionally stopped dead in its tracks, but rarely boring. As I've related to many friends, I'm still figuring out *what* I will be when I finally grow up. Join me on the journey and we'll determine together how I've managed on the quest. I'll appreciate having your company. Thanks.

1

GETTING YOUNGEST
EARLY

Unintended consequences led to my first "youngest" tag, when my parents concurred with my school's educators that I should skip the third grade, due to the fact that everyone believed that I simply needed a more challenging learning environment. That is when I first stepped into the role of being "the youngest." It also meant that I would almost assuredly be the youngest student in every grade, beginning with fourth and continuing throughout high school. This transpired in Oak Ridge, Tennessee, after I had completed the second grade, and not long after we had moved from my birthplace of Akron, Ohio.

The lack of jobs in the recession-torn South led to my parents' relocation to Akron, and also led to my parents' return to the South, when the "Secret City" was born in 1944. My youngest streak continued there through the celebrations of wartime victories in Europe, and the massively exuberant celebration that occurred when Japan surrendered unconditionally following the dropping of the Oak Ridge-assisted atomic bombs. We then moved a few miles west to my dad's home place of Harriman, where I graduated from high school, having experienced the idyllic, small town life, where everyone knew everyone. We weren't wealthy, but my brother, Gary and I never wanted for anything. However, having graduated, I was ready to move on, so my parents gave their permission and signed the necessary paperwork so that I could join the U.S. Air Force following graduation.

Doing so addressed several situations: full independence, the ability to get married, and earning the G.I. Bill, so that I could attend college following my discharge from the service. After basic training in San Antonio, Texas, I was sent to the San Francisco Bay Area, where I fell in total love with the area and the wonders of the Cali lifestyle. I would later have a brief assignment in Albuquerque, New Mexico, before winding up on a small base just outside of San Antonio.

During my last year at Medina Base (a new facility just outside of San Antonio), I talked to the Special Services officer about starting a base newspaper. I told him I planned to major in journalism, though I possibly exaggerated both my knowledge and my skill level. But, he liked the idea, and transferred me to his section (which also relieved me of my shift responsibilities in communications), and created an office for me in the base library.

Thus, the *Medina Base News* was born, and I began work on my first issue in my journalism career. Now, I've made many faux pas, but one of the most embarrassing occurred during that period, even though I didn't realize it until months later when I was in college. A visiting general was touring the base, and my boss, who was a colonel, brought his distinguished guest over and introduced me as the editor of the newly conceived newspaper. When the general asked me how many pages I was planning for my first issue, I said, "Not sure yet, sir, probably seven or eight." He shot me a quizzical look, said nothing more and continued on his tour. I still blush whenever I think of my exchange with the general. As anyone who has even the most rudimentary knowledge about printing knows, there are only even numbers of pages. That nugget of information would become an integral part of my journalism future.

The Accelerated College Experience

My Air Force enlistment was for four years, but, because I was leaving the service to attend college, I could get a discharge six months early. Thus, when my military service concluded on Dec. 31, 1957, I headed to Knoxville to enroll in the University of Tennessee's Winter Quarter, starting in January 1958.

After adjusting my few semester hours from my correspondence and junior college courses, I plotted an aggressive course of study to finish as quickly as possible. It wasn't that I didn't want to enjoy the "college experience," but I needed to get through and into the workforce as quickly as possible. I took 18 to 21 hours of classes each quarter, year-round, until I graduated in August of 1960.

We lived in Sutherland Village, the married housing complex, in the shadows of the elite Sequoyah Hills. However, our complex was the aesthetic opposite of that swanky neighborhood. But everyone who lived there was in the same drab boat. When we welcomed our first son, Sam, on September 1, 1958, we moved into a more luxurious (I am using that word sarcastically here) two-bedroom apartment.

The $135 monthly GI bill payments didn't stretch too far so I worked a lot of part-time jobs, doing whatever I could whenever I could. I worked for two straight years as a uniformed attendant at the Tennessee Valley Agricultural and Industrial Fair, held each year between the summer and fall quarters. I was able to clock in for more than 150 hours during the 11-day event. The $2 per hour I made came in very handy. I worked in the U.S. Post Office at Christmas time, sold pots and pans door-to-door, and other odd jobs when I could find one.

After getting into my journalism courses, I was approached by a relatively recent graduate of the UT School of Journalism, Jack Johnson, who wanted to start a neighborhood weekly newspaper called, *The West Knoxville News.* He offered me the job as editor, (it was a part-time gig), and said he could pay me the whopping sum of $50 a week. I jumped on it, and spent the rest of my time at UT serving in that role.

Johnson and I became fast friends, and not long after I left, he sold the newspaper and moved to Nashville to break into the music publishing business. We would get together for drinks when I visited Nashville for a Tennessee Press Association meeting, and he would always have some "big deal" just around the corner he wanted to discuss, but none seemed to be the "home run" many in Nashville sought. On one of those trips, he was excited about a new artist he had just signed, who he said was Black, but was going to rock the country music world. I nodded while figuratively rolling my eyes, and assuming it was another one of Johnson's pie-in-the-sky dreams. Soon after, I began hearing about Charley Pride, Johnson's artist who totally rocked both the country and the music worlds for many years. When I moved to Nashville full-time a few decades later, Johnson called me from his yacht in Florida. He said he hoped we might do some business to-gether. When he passed away in 2008, he was cited as an icon in the country music world, where he had also worked with the legendary Ronnie Milsap and T. G. Sheppard. He was a perfect illustration of what dreaming "big" could mean in Nashville.

Though my academic career was accelerated, I had many inspiring experiences. At that time, the School of Journalism was located within the UT College of Business, a relatively small and new operation (having become a "School" in 1957 after starting as a "Department of Journalism" in 1947). The director, though he was called Dean by many, was former journalist Willis C. Tucker. A crusty, hard-driv-ing, imposing leader who didn't tolerate incompetence of any kind, Tucker was destined to become a legend. Students who enrolled in UT's J-school 25 years later would note that they knew of Tucker's legacy and influence before they ever arrived on campus.

Tucker was ably assisted in his transformation of the College by three professors: the sharp-penciled, formidable John Lain, a teacher who demanded excellence in writing and editing skills; James Kalshoven, who nurtured feature writers as though they were potential Pulitzer Prize winners, and Frank Thornburg, who focused on advertising and public relations, two disciplines which would evolve and become more invaluable in the future. Being slightly older than my contem-poraries, I developed affable mentorships with these professors while lapping up all the knowledge possible. This time around I was a more devoted student than I had been in high school. I was honored with the first Ernie Pyle (named for the famed WWII war correspondent) Award, which was given to the top journalism graduate, the Sigma

Delta Chi Outstanding Senior Award and was inducted into the Kappa Tau Alpha Honor Society. (It probably goes without saying that those were the extent of my fraternal activities, as I was in no position to participate in the costs or shenanigans of social fraternities.)

Though rushed, I had some unforgettable learning experiences in Knoxville. One of the advantages of majoring in journalism was that it offered many elective hours, under the premise that a journalist should be well-versed in a broad range of subjects. I was able to pick up minors in history and political science, both of which exposed me to some dynamic teachers, particularly during the summer quarters when visiting professors from other universities would teach. Dr. James Davidson, who later became Dean of Newcomb College at Tulane University, was a perfect example. He taught political science classes during two different summer quarters and was a commanding communicator. He had the ability to frame abstract subjects in such a way as to make them seem somewhat elementary, despite their complexity. The classes were small, usually with six underclassmen like myself, and nine graduate students. We often met in the evening at Davidson's apartment, extending our enlightening discussions over a beer or two.

One not so great an experience came during my last quarter at UT. I had already taken the job in Sevier County working at the two newspapers, living in Sevierville, and had scheduled my classes for Mondays, Wednesdays and Fridays, so that I could work full-time during the other days. After I had already completed registration, one of my classes was canceled due to lack of adequate enrollment. Suddenly,

I had to find an open class with availability that met from 10-11 on M-W-F mornings. The single class which fit that criteria was an upper level Psychology class. When I arrived on the second day of classes, there were no textbooks, and I was the only undergraduate student; the situation immediately felt a bit ominous. The lecturer spoke English with a thick German accent, so he was somewhat difficult to understand. That made little difference, though, because I quickly realized that the subject matter was almost incomprehensible. Luckily, I discovered that students could earn extra credit by volunteering for experimental activities at night. I signed up right away. The first "class" was a study that would proceed if one could be hypnotized. I needed it so desperately, that I faked it the first few times. By the end of the quarter, however, I couldn't discern whether I was acting or whether I was being partially hypnotized? In any event, I received enough extra credit to earn the one and only "D" of my college career. I don't know when I was more proud of a grade!

Despite not having much time for socializing, I did establish some friendships with fellow students. In journalism, Duren Cheek and Bob Gilbert, who headed up the statewide offices of UPI and AP, respectively, became friends with whom I interacted over the years. A fellow Air Force vet, Charlie McCarthy, and I shared a writing class offered by the English Department and became chummy. He cut quite a figure with his "James Dean-esque" looks, mannerisms and attitude. I quickly saw that I would never be in his league from a writing standpoint (few would), but we had an easy camaraderie that stretched over several years. Because his given name was better known as that of the famous wooden dummy who sat on the knee of renowned ventriloquist Edgar Bergen, McCarthy decided it would be more advantageous to use a family nickname for his professional endeavors. As Cormac McCarthy, he became known as a supremely accomplished Pulitzer Prize-winning novelist, screenwriter and playwright.

We would get together occasionally after he returned from his service stint and settled in rural Blount County, just outside of Knoxville. He lived with his new English wife, Annie DeLisle, frugally (as he was virtually penniless) in a barn, where he could write in semi-seclusion. After the marriage faltered in the '70s, McCarthy decamped for the Southwest. Years later, I thoroughly enjoyed dining at Annie's, an atmospheric boîte serving Italian dishes to the 24-or-so patrons it could accommodate, while strains of jazz music wafted in from its minuscule courtyard. DeLisle had become an entrepreneur under the guidance of Knoxville's visionary developer and tastemaker Kristopher Kendrick, who pioneered the revitalization of "Old City" in 1983. Last I heard, McCarthy was hanging out with scientists and other geniuses at New Mexico's Santa Fe Institute, and DeLisle had retired to Florida.

Finally, being a sports fiend, my time at UT as a student coincided with two uninspiring years on the football field for the Volunteers. They fell first to Florida State, a school that had been a women-only college a few seasons earlier. The humiliating loss to the Seminoles was followed by a brutal loss against neighboring University of Chattanooga in 1958, which engendered a riot. Yes, a serious riot with arrests. There was one totally triumphant game: as if by magic, the 1959 team prevented a two-point conversion attempt by the Billy Cannon-led LSU Tigers, and beat the number one team in the nation,

14 to 13. A stop-action image of that unbelievable play near the end zone graced the UT Athletic Department offices for as long as I can remember, a stirring reminder of a miraculous moment in collegiate football history. It was a photograph for the ages. I hope it's still there.

Today, as I write this, my blood still runs deeply and eternally Orange. Thanks, UT.

2

THE YOUNGEST EDITOR

1960: Sevier County News-Record and Gatlinburg Press

Until *Publisher's Auxiliary*, a national journalism publication, was preparing to run a story about me being the youngest editor in the U.S., I was not aware of it until they contacted me about their story. At 23, I was working as the editor of the *Sevier County News-Record* and managing editor of the *Gatlinburg Press*.

The *News-Record* was a typical county weekly newspaper published in Sevierville, Tennessee. The *Gatlinburg Press* and the publishing plant were located in Gatlinburg, Tennessee, the gateway city of the Great Smoky Mountains National Park (the most visited national park in the U.S.).

The story of my arrival at these locations began at UT. The dapper Bill Postlewaite was the publisher of both newspapers. His entry into the business in Tennessee was a story in and of itself. A WWII veteran, his father owned and ran a printing operation in the Chicago, Illinois area. Postlewaite packed up his wife, Gretchen, and with a station wagon full of loads of type and other equipment, they headed out in search of a place to start a printing operation and a newspaper. While traveling through Tennessee, they experienced car trouble in Gatlinburg and found themselves there for two extra nights. With nothing else to do while waiting for repairs, they began checking around and determined there was no printing operation or newspaper serving the small city of Gatlinburg. Postlewaite had a vision about what the city could become when the WWII veterans returned, and how the improving economy would allow people to travel and visit this park in the eastern U.S. So, he and Gretchen decided to set up shop and begin their printing operation with a small weekly publication called the *Gatlinburg Press*.

As Gatlinburg grew, hotels were built, printing needs expanded, and Postlewaite's operation became very successful. Later he purchased the county weekly, the *Sevier County News-Record*, which was headquartered in the county seat, Sevierville. His printing plant in Gatlinburg published both newspapers. There was an office, an office manager and social editor, a part-time photographer, and an ad sales lady located in Sevierville, but Bill wanted an editor to become the face of the newspaper there.

He drove to Knoxville to meet with Glenn McNeil, president of the Tennessee Press Association, headquartered on the University of Tennessee campus. He asked McNeil if there were any promising young students who might be interested in coming to edit his newspaper. They discussed it with Dean Tucker and Julian Harriss, head of public relations for UT. Both recommended me as I was a slightly more mature student. Plus, I had worked part-time in the public relations office at UT (for the grand sum of $0.60 per hour), so I had gotten to know Harriss and others on the staff. A meeting was set up in the UT offices where Mr. Postlewaite and I talked for more than an hour. He outlined his vision and said he would like to hire me as managing editor. He wanted me to relocate to Sevierville before my graduation in a few months, and upon graduation, he would make me editor of the publication if things were going well. I would start at a certain salary, which would increase upon graduation.

I wanted to talk about his proposal with my family and think about it. Having grown up in a small East Tennessee town, I wasn't certain that I wanted to begin my career in yet another small East Tennessee town. A major factor that influenced my decision-making process was that the salary Postlewaite offered was higher than any of the daily newspapers in Tennessee were paying at that time. I decided to take his offer, and moved my young family to a rented house in Sevierville. I was a managing editor!

There was already an office and a desk there, so I dove in and got right to work. Pretty soon, my assistant/secretary/social editor/local contact, Eula Catlett, acclimated me to the Sevier County "way of life." The strong Republican leanings of the county were not that much different from the county where I grew up, little more than 60 miles away. Roane County was similar in some ways, but as I learned, there were vast differences between the inhabitants of those two places. Sevier County was a bonafide example of Appalachia. While both counties are mountainous, Sevier County residents appeared much more isolated, as if they were less willing to accept an outsider coming into their midst. They weren't negative, they were simply skeptical and curious about newcomers. After living there, working there, getting to know people, becoming a part of the community, and reporting on many aspects of daily life there, I felt total acceptance. I had truly become one of them. And, if an outsider came in and attacked me, the Sevier Countians would have been the first to stand up and defend me.

Some customs were also different. For example, our staff photographer only worked part-time because she and her sister also owned the local flower shop. They generated a great deal of their income through activities related to funerals, which were highly significant occasions in Sevier County. Not only were flowers abundant, but there were many photographs of the arrangements. It was not unusual when I visited someone's home for a story, farther out in the country particularly, for there to be two or three framed funeral images prominently displayed. One might be of a wedding, and one might be of a funeral. Those were two occasions where all of the folks in the family would gather dressed in their Sunday best.

Sevier County also was unique in having a city like Gatlinburg. The property owners in Gatlinburg were regular Sevier County folks, but they were very astute from a business standpoint. Many worked with developers who came to build hotels, but they never sold them their land. Instead, they leased the land, which would command a certain price plus a specific percentage of the business's income. The ownership of much of the land in downtown Gatlinburg and its closely surrounding areas was held by a few old-line families, who maintained tight control of their property. Interestingly enough, during those days, business boomed from May through October. But, in November, many of the businesses would shut down until late spring to accommodate the mass exodus of property owners and hotel operators headed to Florida for the winter. For example, the *Gatlinburg Press* circulation, which was about 75,000 readers per week during the summer months, dropped to 1,100 per week during the winter months.

* * *

While I made the drive between Sevierville and Gatlinburg at least twice a week, the natural beauty of the 4.5 miles of the Foothills Parkway between Pigeon Forge and Gatlinburg never got old. I still consider it one of the most glorious drives anywhere in the world.

* * *

As I settled into my new job and surroundings, I was able to arrange my schedule at UT so that I attended classes in the mornings on Monday, Wednesday, and Friday. This enabled me to commute to the university three days a week while spending the rest of my time working. I liked to have all my stories written and edited by the end of business on Monday, so that the typesetters could start setting that night. Then, on Tuesday mornings, I would go to our printing operation in Gatlinburg, compose the headlines and create the newspaper's layout. Printing would take place on Tuesday with the paper ready for circulation early on Wednesday.

Without much detailed guidance from my publisher, I dove head-long into covering things that I knew about, such as Sevierville City Council, the Sevier County Commission, the Sevier County school board, and other important areas of governance as I became aware of them. I would attend those meetings, draft my story, check my spelling, and turn in my work.

Reprinted below is an example of a rare, but serious crime story, the first murder case I covered as part of my community beat:

> *His entrance to the courtroom was quite a show, as he sauntered in after the judge had been introduced and literally nodded his head to give his figurative acknowledgment to the judge, the jury, the prosecutor, and any others who were lucky enough to be in his presence.*
>
> *He was Ray Jenkins, the famed defense lawyer from Knoxville who first received national attention as a lawyer who was central in dethroning the infamous Senator Joe McCarthy on national television.*
>
> *He was gracing Sevier County to defend a prominent Gatlinburg businessman, Carl Fancher, who was accused of murdering his wife and his mother-in-law.*

To see this man with a larger-than-life reputation perform in a courtroom made for an enduring experience.

The prosecutor had presented a clear case for Fancher shooting his wife five times as she tried to escape by going up the stairs in their home and then shooting his mother-in-law twice. The accused was a native Sevier Countian from a prominent family; the victims were both originally from Cincinnati, Ohio. The defense didn't really dispute the facts of the case as it started its presentation.

Jenkins called about a dozen character witnesses. He would ask them if they knew Mr. Fancher as an "honorable, God-fearing, reputable citizen of Gatlinburg and Sevier County?" (Versions of "Oh, yes, yes, yes," were the standard replies.) Or was he a "mean, villainous, violent character?" (Answers were versions of "My goodness, no, no, no.") Over and over, the witnesses were part of the orchestrated martyrization of Fancher.

I kept waiting for additional information, maybe a startling fact or a hint of something which might suggest that what transpired didn't happen. Nope, the character witnesses were basically it . . . including the drama of the questioner, attorney Jenkins. The jury was charged by the presiding judge. They left but, in just over an hour, returned with their verdict . . . guilty as charged on all counts. Then came their recommended sentence: 18 months of probation. No one seemed surprised.

Since there were apparently no family members there to speak for the victims, no one seemed displeased, including the prosecuting attorney. All parties were acknowledged and thanked by the famed lawyer, who had consented to journey the 20 or so miles from Knoxville to grace us with his presence.

I didn't feel "graced," but later in life, when I worked for a governor who refused to allow executions of sentenced prisoners, who were all poor, and mostly Black, I was proud. My faith in our criminal justice system was not destroyed but seriously shaken by the Fancher trial. I didn't demonize Ray Jenkins. He did his job, for which I am certain that he was handsomely rewarded.

Another interesting thing occurred after my first few weeks at the newspapers. The superintendent of schools met with my publisher and suggested that perhaps the paper should return to its former approach of simply printing the minutes furnished from the meeting rather than have someone (me) cover and report about the meeting. The superintendent objected to having members quoted and questions and issues raised. To his credit, Mr. Postlewaite listened courteously and said that this was a "new day" and that the coverage would continue, and that we would be as fair and accurate as possible.

That was a seminal moment in my career. My boss said that we would proceed with using the best journalism practices. I never had a policy or position edited by Mr. Postlewaite, even if we discussed things later.

 I was impressed and thrilled that the Postlewaites attended my August graduation from UT. I enjoyed introducing them to my parents, and was delighted that my father and Bill had a beer together on that sweltering August afternoon.

It was much later that I realized how fortunate I was to be in a position of having the freedom and support that I enjoyed during my first job out of college. I was a seasoned 23, having been through the Air Force and college, but I was still a rookie. I started as news editor in March, graduated from UT in August, was promoted to editor in September, and, by November, was writing my own editorials and political endorsements. For example, we published two editorials with endorsements for the 1960 presidential election. My editorial endorsed young John F. Kennedy, the Democrat, while Mr. Postlewaite produced a separate editorial endorsing Richard Nixon, the Republican nominee.

My candidate won nationally, but I certainly didn't have an inflated ego about my endorsement. Vice President Nixon carried Sevier County with 87% of the vote. I also learned that this was the typical party breakdown for most elections in the heavily GOP county.

Pushing the Schools into the 20th Century

One of the major changes that occurred during my time in Sevier County was within the school system. I supported an overhaul of the system and gave credence to that by reporting on the school board's actions. My reporting shone a light on that board—not that they were necessarily doing things wrong—but it showed the public what was really happening at those meetings. The existing "good ole boy" system was largely to blame. A school board member could run his district as if it were his own personal fiefdom. He could hire whomever he wanted as bus drivers and janitors. More than half of the teachers in Sevier County did not hold college degrees. The predominant schools, as well as the ones in the outlying areas, were one-room schoolhouses. There was one teacher, in one room, instructing grades one through eight. The prevailing aspiration in Sevier County at the time was to get through eighth grade and get the kids back to work. There was talk of consolidating school districts and schools, which was bitterly opposed by many people, particularly the school board members themselves. A parent (Gene Hickey, more about her below) initiated a request to the parent–teacher association of the State Department of Education to come and assess the school system. Hickey was part of an organization called Sevier County Citizens for Better Schools, chaired by the distinguished Dr. William Broady. In the newspapers, we publicized the group and supported the proposed changes for Sevier County's schools.

The ultimate report which the Department of Education issued could only be described as beyond scathing. It outlined the many issues and shortcomings of the county's entire educational system, and produced a litany of recommendations for extensive improvements. The full report was reprinted in our newspapers, covering several pages, from top to bottom. For emphasis, we reversed the markers between the columns, which gave the copy a feeling reminiscent of carving one sees on tombstones.

It was definitely a time of upheaval in local education. The resulting fallout of the school report led to six of the seven school board members being defeated in the next election. The newly elected members were supported by Sevier County Citizens for Better Schools. The only incumbent who survived the election was Bill Cox of Gatlinburg, a good man who had no opponent.

One of the significant results was the closure of the one-room schoolhouses. The school board couldn't change every outdated practice overnight, but there was serious education reform, which included the integration of schools. With, perhaps, 40 "Negro" children in the entire county, their integration, while done quietly and without fanfare, would eventually provoke a reaction by the Ku Klux Klan (more to come later about this issue).

Getting an Equal Tax Base

Another change was the reappraisal of property, with the acceptance of a standardized and professional way to accomplish that task. The updated property value system, which would develop a tax base to support better schools and other improvements, would be instituted in a more fair and progressive manner.

Sevier County Judge Ray L. Reagan knew that things needed to change and that the county needed to have a tax base with a taxation system that would provide funds for progress. Central to his campaign, and then to his mission from day one as county judge, was to create new jobs in Sevier County. The need for jobs was an issue he knew well. Before he became county judge, he had commuted to Knoxville and back to work.

Judge Reagan also established the first-ever industrial park in the county. He looked for ways to improve and enhance tourism, which was already a job-creating entity in Gatlinburg (and later in Pigeon Forge and Sevierville, as well). But, he also recognized the need for an aggressive approach in order to get things done in Sevier County. Taxed-based support, raised equitably, was imperative.

At the time, Tennessee had passed laws regarding the reappraisal of property which specified using professional appraisers. To his credit, the Sevier County tax assessor, also an elected official, publicly affirmed that he would accept professional appraisals. In other parts of Tennessee, counties resisted these changes. So, in this case, it was important for Judge Reagan to start encouraging candidates for county court who would support the changes.

As an example of the Judge's adept manner in handling people, right after state law mandated the reappraisal of property, residents came in droves to complain about their increased valuation and how that would ultimately impact their tax bill. Judge Reagan often had wealthy county landowners seated with him in his office as guests. On more than several occasions, I overheard any one of these entitled land-owners say, for example, "Jim (or whatever the complainer's first name was), I'll buy your property for that appraised value right now, if you'll take it."

It was unexpected how quickly the protests subsided, and eventually, the hue-and-cry turned to the next unpopular issue. Few landowners really became that upset. It was a way of saying that property values do increase, and it depends on your point-of-view as to what that valuation means.

Judge Reagan never campaigned against anyone, but he let it be known who would be favorable to the revised, upgraded way of conducting business in Sevier County. It took more than one election cycle, but eventually, the court was situated to proceed with many other worthwhile projects, in addition to the industrial park. Among the infrastructure improvements that moved ahead were an airport and a new county hospital. Judge Reagan had the foresight to position the county to take advantage of both the growth on the horizon and the jobs that naturally accompanied economic expansion.

Ski Gatlinburg

Another major story which occurred during my time as editor was the introduction of snow skiing in Gatlinburg, which was developed by an outside company in 1961 and operational by 1963. The Gatlinburg paper covered the story in detail, along with the expected lawsuits involved in bringing snow-covered slopes to town. Skiing seemed like an excellent method for enhancing the meager number of choices on Gatlinburg's wintertime activity list. There were a few holiday events which occurred annually, but nothing substantial.

Because it didn't snow much in the Smokies, snow-making equipment could powder the steep inclines surrounding Gatlinburg in order to develop a new fall and winter-based economy, with new jobs and fresh economic opportunities. The mayor, the Chamber of Commerce, and the city manager were highly supportive of the project. Because this expansion represented a significant change, they required that the highest-quality equipment be installed for such infrastructure as the ski lifts.

Others didn't warm to the idea of skiing as much. They were comfortable with the Gatlinburg they had. Already a substantial tourist draw during the half of the year, there were many for whom the seasonal time-frame seemed just right. Skiing alleviated the natural break in the action, as it created a year-round attraction. The city soon developed a successful Christmas Village experience, too. This already popular mountain town was ascending to an even higher elevation on the ladder of success.

Flooding Plagued Sevier County, Sevierville

I was totally shocked the first time we had serious flooding in Sevier County. During one occurrence, I was actually in a motor boat with a photographer riding up and down the main streets in Sevierville. Not surprisingly, the damage to roads throughout the country was substantial. Most of our "country roads" were graded, not paved, and kept passable using loads of gravel. One of the best promises any candidate for county Road Superintendent could make was that of pouring more gravel on designated roadways. The flood I experienced was in 1961, during the early days of the Kennedy administration. Because President Kennedy was boosted in his Democratic Primary bid with a win in West Virginia, he had pledged to address the problems and poverty of the Appalachian region of the country. Soon after the floods, the White House dispatched a delegation of bright, young men to Sevier County to meet with officials in order to determine how to remedy the devastation.

After touring much of the county, and surveying the extensive road damage in particular, the head of the delegation from Washington, said to John Rimel, the Road Superintendent: "Mr. Rimel, we have seen the devastation throughout your county. What would you estimate, as a ballpark figure, the amount of the damages?"

Rimel pursed his lips, scratched his head, and thought for a moment or two, before replying: "Lord, son, h'its a sight."

Hearing what may have sounded like a foreign language, the young man was momentarily rendered speechless.

Some relief funds did arrive, but primarily the presidential team's visit kicked off a series of studies with the Tennessee Valley Authority (TVA), which would, in a few years, lead to the re-routing of some streams and other work that would eliminate the disastrous flooding in Sevier County.

Tragedy Engulfs a Nation

On the 22nd of November, 1963, a tragic event impacted the world. America's 35th President, John Fitzgerald Kennedy, was assassinated in Dallas, Texas. As stunned as most everyone was, I turned to my typewriter to document what I saw going on, and then recorded my impressions. Here are those two pieces:

Our Country Mourns the Death of a President

Cast into a position of awesome power and responsibility that carried with it the God-like control of life and death on this earth, the President of the United States gave his life for all of us Friday afternoon in Dallas.

John Fitzgerald Kennedy died at the age of 46 as the result of an assassin's bullet during a parade down the streets of Dallas on November 22nd. That same day, Lyndon B. Johnson *became the 36th president of our nation.*

A little bit of all of us died as life ebbed from the body of our dynamic leader; hearts were heavy with sorrow for his family; prayers were breathed to give President Johnson the necessary strength to carry on the affairs of the nation.

What was the reaction in Sevier County? Eighty percent of the people here are Republicans. How did we react?

I was sitting in Jack Stewart's Drug Store in Sevierville when the announcement came that our president was dead. A stunned silence engulfed the store. No one spoke. It seemed no one breathed. One young man from Knoxville slammed his fist on a table, demonstrating the frustrating anger that I'm sure all of us felt. One waitress seemed to be fighting to hold back tears.

There was little movement, but a deaf man at one of the tables, I believe, could feel what had happened. He nodded his head in acknowledgment when the person next to him wrote what happened on her napkin.

The bright sunshine outside reflected sad faces; the town seemed almost void of noise. When you talked to someone or heard someone talking, it was about the same thing:

"That's terrible about the president."
"I can't believe it."
"Who could have done such a terrible thing?"

On and on it went. Life continued to go on. Even the murder of our president couldn't stop everything though it seemed most moved as if in a stupor, sort of floating along in a horrible nightmare.

The shock and gloom did not lessen over the weekend in Sevier County. Life did go on, but it seemed as if everyone carried out their duties in a zombie-like manner. In motion, without emotion.

The First Baptist Church in Sevierville had a special memorial service Sunday night. Rev. Gordon Greenwell, pastor of the church, led prayers for President Kennedy's family and mourners and for God's help in guiding President Lyndon B. Johnson in his efforts to lead our country. Special prayers were offered in other churches in the county, and Sunday church service attendance ran higher than normal.

Monday was an official day of mourning. The Sevier County Schools were closed, as was the courthouse and all county offices, the U.S. Post Office, and many businesses. Some businesses closed between 11 a.m. and 1 p.m. for the funeral of our late president.

County Judge Ray L. Reagan said he was traveling from industrial meetings in Nashville when he heard the news. "It is shocking and incredible that such a thing could happen in our country, a terrible thing," Judge Reagan said.

Normally it is hard to generalize when speaking about the reactions of a large group of people to any one thing. But in this case, I feel it is different. Talking to people in Sevierville, Pigeon Forge, and Gatlinburg, there was clearly similarity in the way we in Sevier County reacted. The cloud of gloom could not be erased. Groups gathered, attempted to talk of other things, but somehow everything else was insignificant.

The reaction to accused assassin Lee Oswald's murder was also seemingly very general. Though most of us would like to see our president's assassin dead, we were indignant that our civilized way of handling such matters was averted.

Some may recall that Friday, November 22nd, was the first day of winter, the shortest—thus the darkest—day of the year. It was that, plus one of the darkest days in our nation's history. (I got the date of winter wrong, but nobody noticed it, or at least no one brought it to my attention.)

Many Sevier Countians may have gone to Washington, D.C. to attend the funeral for President Kennedy. The only one for sure I heard about was Clyde Ownby, a Sevierville insurance man who took his three sons.

One merchant, Herbert Lawson at the Corner Store, said business was brisk just before the announcement came about the shooting. The stunned hush fell there as elsewhere as the word spread. He said everyone seemed to head for home to find out what had happened. Other merchants reported similar experiences.

On and on the story goes, Sevier Countians, 80% of them Republicans, but first of all 100% Americans.

I also wrote a more personal piece, reflecting the overwhelming emotional turmoil that I experienced that day.

The time is 2:45 p.m. The typewriter looks cold and impersonal on this sunny Friday afternoon. I want to destroy it, destroy something. The president, MY president, is dead, I have just learned. Good edito-

rial policy calls for me to wait before writing anything, cool off; maybe we should never cool off after such a terrible thing.

The cold, impersonal, and tangible typewriter reassures me that the news I have heard is not a dream, though it is almost too unbelievable to comprehend.

The president is dead. At this time, the details are not known; by the time you read this, the assassin may have already been apprehended, but the vile fact is known that our president is dead. My stomach boils with the thoughts of such a cowardly act. I, along with many other people, didn't go along with a lot of the programs that President Kennedy advocated. I still disagree with many of the philosophies this man held and have no apologies . . . but he was MY president; he was YOUR president.

It is a sad and terrible thing, this murder, and our hearts, along with the most beautiful flag in the world will fly at half mast.

The Heroes of Sevier County

No matter the topography, no matter the weather, it's actually the people who make a location unique. I had the pleasure of meeting, working with, and working for some exceptional individuals during the first four years of my career in Sevier County. Here are a few:

Judge Ray L. Reagan

Judge Reagan was one of the signature names in Sevier County that included Ogle, Huskey, Maples, McCarter, and a few others. When one heard the name, you could ask: are you from Sevier County?

The aforementioned Judge Reagan was county judge (what now would be called county mayor) and also served as an entry-level judge for the county. With only slightly more education than high school, but the first in his family to graduate from high school, Reagan was one of the smartest, brightest, and most visionary people I ever met. I considered him a friend, and prized him as a mentor. He had a way of diffusing difficult situations, finding ways for people to get along, and achieving the outcome that he desired, which was usually best for all involved. He loved his county, he loved and respected (and restored) the historic courthouse in which his office was located, and he thoroughly enjoyed being a public servant. In the face of custom, his attitude was that Sevier Countians deserved as good or better than anybody else in the state.

Judge Reagan passed away too soon, at the age of 56 in 1978, while he was still in office, serving his third eight-year term as county judge. He remains a personal hero and an iconic figure who laid the foundation for a modern Sevier County.

Johnny Waters

After a couple of years in Sevier County, my family and I were very lucky to move into the home next door to Johnny Waters and his family. Our kids were of similar age and began to grow up together. Waters was a successful attorney, an active politician, and the son of a wealthy landowner—John B, Waters, Sr., one of the largest landowners in Sevier County. Waters had run for Congress a year before I met him. He was such a promoter that he brought in a live elephant to underscore his Republican campaign. He garnered a lot of attention and ran an excellent race, but could not unseat the long-time incumbent in the First Congressional District.

One of Waters' law school classmates and fraternity brothers was a young man by the name of Howard Baker, Jr. It was through Waters that I met Baker early on. Waters was Baker's campaign manager during his initial run for the U.S. Senate, which he lost. He was also the campaign manager for Baker's second run—a race in which he was victorious with 55% of the vote, thus beginning a public service career of exceptional impact for Tennessee and the U.S.

Waters and I used to sit on lawn chairs in our front yards and discuss politics for hours. Even though I was one of the few Democrats in Sevier County, our political views, while different, were not really so far apart. I think we both came from a base of standing by our values without allowing partisanship to interfere with the right thing to do. He became a wonderful friend and mentor, as well.

Much later, after I had departed Sevier County and was serving in the Tennessee governor's office, and working a lot in Washington, D.C., I received a call from Senator Baker's office. His assistant invited me to meet him for breakfast in the Senate dining room. This was soon after Richard Nixon had defeated Hubert Humphrey to become the

President-elect. During our enjoyable breakfast, Senator Baker looked at me, smiled, and asked how I would feel about Waters becoming Federal co-chairman of the Appalachian Regional Commission. Though totally unprepared for the question, I said that would be the greatest thing since the creation of TVA, or some similar nonsensical comparison.

As the Tennessee governor's representative on the Appalachian Commission, Waters and I enjoyed working together and helping the region, while ensuring that Tennessee received its fair share of funding allocations. Waters was later appointed chairman of the Tennessee Valley Authority. A proud veteran of the U.S. Navy, he was one of the best friends and most trusted confidants that I ever had. His family was very important to him, and we were fortunate to share the same experiences, including a few business and public service ventures. Later in my career, my professional path crossed with his daughter, Cyndy B. Waters, a photographer of note (with a great eye), who became one of the official photographers of the 1982 World's Fair in Knoxville. We still communicate, and I enjoy following her admirable missionary work in Africa, as she continues her award-winning photography career in the U.S.

Jimmie Temple

Jimmie Temple was Johnny Waters' brother-in-law by way of his marriage to Jimmie's sister, Patsy. The Temple family owned one of the large mills in town, making flour in a very lucrative business operation. Temple later ran for, and was elected, as mayor of Sevierville. We worked alongside one another in my reporting of government activities for years.

I remember Temple dropping by my office one day and musing aloud, "I'm thinking about running for re-election as mayor, but nobody has come to me and asked me to run." I remember laughing because the practice at that time was for candidates to place a newspaper ad stating, "Many of my friends and neighbors have come to me asking me to run for this office" or "stand for re-election," and so forth. I told him, "No one necessarily came to any of those candidates asking them anything; it wasn't unusual, but people liked that phrase. So, Jimmie, just because no one asked you to run doesn't mean that a lot of people don't want you to." Needless to say, he ran again, won again, and continued to be an outstanding mayor. The job of the mayor of Sevierville paid a hefty sum of zero. Temple devoted his time to being a public servant, volunteering his ideas, energy and leadership. He was a superb example of many of the folks I came to know who loved their city, county, and the people in it and simply wanted to contribute.

Gene Hickey

The indomitable Eugenia "Gene" Hickey was not a native Sevier Countian and had not resided there long. She arrived there because her husband, John, moved to Sevierville to open a medical practice, one of the few new physicians in a county that desperately needed them. She was extremely invested in the community, particularly in the education of her children and others in Sevier County. As the daughter of a construction contractor growing up, she lived in 13 different cities. With five children of her own, she wanted to settle down in a place with quality schools.

She was a determined sort who may have irritated many people, including me, when I first got to know her. In her late 30s, she was a nurse and a mother who wanted to get things done. She was a serious influencer behind-the-scenes because women didn't step out and take the lead that much in those days.

After good-naturedly hounding me a lot, we began to talk seriously about the county's school system. We quickly discovered that I was an ally of hers. I didn't publicly promote our kindred-ship because she didn't want to be promoted; she was far more interested in results. Following a long and involved effort by many people, we were able to get the State Department of Education to conduct an in-depth study of the county's schools, assess their status and follow with recommendations for dramatic improvement.

Many communities fought the closing of their one-room schools because they were "their schools" and because their communities were linked to, and recognized, by those schools. It was a major change that needed to occur. And it did occur.

As recounted above, the energy and activity of the Sevier County Citizens for Better Schools was inspired, encouraged and energized by the little lady who wouldn't listen to "no."

Hickey was also instrumental in securing a new library for Sevier County.

Following my departure from Sevier County, I moved to Atlanta and then back to Knoxville, where I was heading up the University of Tennessee's news bureau. Mrs. Hickey made an appointment with me to discuss a project she was working on. She wanted to talk about contracting with me to work part-time to help secure funds for a new library. I accepted the challenge, and worked after hours and on weekends, to formulate and implement a plan.

At that time, Sevier County's single library was located inside the Masonic Temple building where it barely covered an entire floor. Its book collection was paltry, its hours limited, and it had no professional librarians. From my time as head of the Cancer Society in Sevier County, I knew that one could raise around $3,500 with a solid, professional fundraising effort, or do just a little and still raise about $2,500. Hickey's goal was an astounding $30,000, which would represent the necessary private funds to be paired with city, county, state and federal funds.

We created the Sevier County Foundation and I convinced my friend, Johnny Waters to serve as chairman of the effort. Appealing to long-time Sevier County residents, we received generous gifts honoring parents, spouses, loved ones, and the dearly departed. The money rolled in: we raised more than $37,000. The Appalachian Regional Commission contributed additional, unexpected dollars, so that we had enough, over and above the construction costs, to set up a small endowment and buy more books than originally envisioned. They were able to construct one of the finest libraries of its time for a county of that size in the Volunteer State, if not the country. (*When Waters was appointed as the Federal head of the Appalachian Regional Commission five years later, while I was Tennessee's representative on the operating committee, his staff and my fellow state members got a bit tired of hearing us tell and then re-tell the Sevier County Library story, which demonstrated the ARC's ability to assist in creating excellence in unexpected ways.*)

Hickey remained a leader later in life. She was elected to the school board and continued to push for better schools. She was quite a force; though it was true that she irritated some people as much as she encouraged and inspired others. To this day, I give an enormous amount of credit to the energy, tenacity, and sheer determination of Gene Hickey. Sevier County is a far better place because of her dedication, single-minded devotion and unbridled enthusiasm.

Hubert Bebb

Bebb, a Cornell-educated architect, was responsible for many of Sevier County's early quality structures, such as the convention center, the city hall, and some hotels in the quaint village of Gatlinburg. An Illinois native who moved to Tennessee in 1950, he also designed the Sevier County Library and the county's first hospital.

Bebb once appeared before the County Court (now called County Commission), to make a presentation about the importance of implementing county-wide zoning. The response was not encouraging. In fact, he was called a "communist" and told that he couldn't "come and tell people how they were going to use their property." He was almost physically, if not psychologically, driven out of the room. Sevier County wasn't quite ready for a brilliant architect like Hubert Bebb just yet.

Eventually, Bebb would be responsible for bringing in some zoning controls. Along with City Manager Judd Mynatt, another outsider, they advanced a forward-looking approach in the city in order to maintain the "mountain village atmosphere" of Gatlinburg, wherever and whenever possible. The Gatlinburg that exists today is largely due to the influence of Bebb and Mynatt, along with the legendary Bill Mills, the city's visionary mayor.

Gatlinburg Power Trio

There were three men who made up the Gatlinburg power trio during my time there. One was W.W. (Judd) Mynatt who was raised in Elizabethton, in upper East Tennessee, and attended Milligan College. The city council of Gatlinburg hired him as the city manager, a position he held for many years. Mynatt was instrumental in setting quality standards for signage and similar controls throughout the small, prosperous city.

Another member of the trio was Bill Mills. A native Sevier Countian and president of the Bank of Gatlinburg, Mills was a genteel Southerner with a mountain touch. Soft spoken, he represented the city admirably, working quietly behind-the-scenes with the city council, to maintain quality as the city developed.

The third member of that trio was Zeno Wall. To describe Wall as an unstoppable ball of fire, was really an understatement—no kidding. Born in Mississippi, he attended high school in North Carolina before enrolling in Wake Forest University. Wall initially moved to Tennessee to work for the American Enka Company, a rayon fiber manufacturer. Mayor Mills helped recruit him as the director of the Gatlinburg Chamber of Commerce. He was well-known across the state, and throughout the region. He did an extraordinary job of "selling" Gatlinburg as a convention location. We became friends and golfing buddies at the Gatlinburg Country Club, which, oddly enough, is located in Pigeon Forge.

These three heroes, along with architect Bebb, brought the energy and vision to instill high standards and values in both design and zoning. Some residents lobbied for more garish signage, clamoring for neon everywhere because they thought it would attract greater attention to their businesses. Many resisted change for decades. It took the quiet, iron will and committed foresight of Mayor Mills to recruit forward-thinking "outsiders" who could bring their expertise to bear in crafting a classic, inviting, attractive foundation on which to shape the "Gateway to the Smoky Mountains."

Fred Atchley

A fixture in Nashville as the state representative from Sevier County, Fred Atchley was elected numerous times. When he occasionally lost his two-year post, he was usually hired by the legislative staff to help out in the biennial and then the annual sessions. Atchley's remarkable resilience saw him elected for the first time in 1949 and he went on to serve 22 of the next 30 years, ending his career in 1978. He would kiddingly say the voters allowed him to rest for stretches along the way.

Atchley was a quiet, soft spoken, highly effective legislator. He got along well with members from both sides of the aisle, and, as the representative of one of the state's leading tourism revenue producers, he generally got whatever he wanted and Sevier County needed each session. Once or twice I joined some of the Sevier County office holders to visit Nashville, where we were hosted by Atchley. Many of them had a ritual in Atchley's suite at the Andrew Jackson Hotel: they would strip down to their underwear, smoke cigars, drink alcohol and beer, and play poker. They relaxed with a little bit of misbehaving while on their guys' trips. No harm, no foul, and no reporting by me on those particular activities.

Atchley taught me one of my most lasting political lessons. After I departed Sevier County and was working in the governor's office, I ran into Atchley in the State Capitol building one day. Delighted to see him, I exclaimed: "Fred, I see you are running without opposition this year." He answered: "No, that's not true. I always have opposition. It just so happens that I don't have an opponent this year." I have shared that particular bit of unsolicited, correcting wisdom with more politicians than I can count.

What Leaders Did

There had long been an attitude of malaise and resistance in Appalachia, as if people were thinking, "We don't really deserve better than this. If it was good enough for me; it'll be good enough for my kids." All of these heroes were instrumental in altering that attitude. That was the story of what I saw leaders attempting to accomplish in Sevier County. Blithely accepting the status quo wasn't the only choice. They could pursue loftier goals. And, these heroes were among the ones who led the way. I was happy to be a small part of this, and thankful for the opportunity to both report on, and be a cheerleader for, their many admirable quests.

The Hairstyle and the KKK

The photo wasn't necessarily flattering, but the hairstyle made it easy to pinpoint precisely when it was taken. That wouldn't have been particularly important, except that a *Life* magazine writer was showing me that my picture had been printed on the front page of the *Fiery Cross,* the national publication of the infamous Ku Klux Klan (KKK).

The article, written from the KKK's jaundiced viewpoint, was certainly not a song of praise. I was labeled everything from an n-lover to a communist, while being summed up as the scum of the earth. From my perspective, however, I found the piece rather flattering. As we talked over lunch in Atlanta, the writer shared the mind-blowing moments he had experienced while preparing a major cover story about the Klan. Our discussion triggered a flood of memories related to my own KKK encounters. The last encounter I had with members of that group, which I hadn't even categorized as an encounter, was documented by the photo. The reason I knew exactly when the photo was taken was that a year earlier, I was transitioning from a crew cut to letting my hair grow out. Those of you who experienced the mid-'60s will clearly recall that it was a particularly unkempt-looking period, when one had the worst of both hair worlds. It was during this time, when, as editor of the *Gatlinburg Press* and the *Sevier County News-Record,* I received a call from two "interns" from the University of Tennessee's School of Journalism. Using the ruse of a "class project," they said they were interviewing recent UT journalism grads, who had "been successful." Well, that was all my ego needed to hear. I invited them to come to Gatlinburg whenever they could.

When two, clean-cut young men arrived for their appointment several days later, they seemed a bit nervous, but I wrote their demeanor off to being young and inexperienced. My friendly banter about UT professors didn't seem to put them at ease, nor did they show any recognition of the names I mentioned. At the end of our brief meeting, it took them seven fumbling tries to get one decent Polaroid photo of me to accompany their "paper." They quickly departed, and I never gave them another thought.....until I saw that issue of the *Fiery Cross* in the hands of the *Life* magazine correspondent. It surprised me that the KKK would go to that much trouble for a single photo. Regardless, I felt slightly uneasy about it.

The trail that precipitated the "photo session" began one Saturday morning when two rather nondescript guys appeared at the newspaper office in Sevierville. They wanted to purchase posters and "possibly some advertising" for an upcoming event. When I found out that they were from nearby Blount County and were henchmen of the KKK, I told them that we would not accept either their printing business or their advertising. They seemed to take my response in stride, said okay, and quickly left.

It was then that I made a grave journalistic error. You see, it was 1964, the times were quite turbulent with racial issues looming large across the nation; America increasingly felt like a tinderbox ready to ignite. The KKK's motivation for moving into Sevier County was the Board of Education's recent decision to integrate the county's schools, a move which the papers had vigorously supported with extremely forceful editorials. Sevier County's population was more than 99% white at the time that the KKK came to call. In fact, there was only one

Black family residing in the entire area; they lived north of Sevierville, and the mother of the household taught school in neighboring Knox County. Had she been working in Sevier County, she would have been one of the very few teachers there who held a master's degree.

My reaction that Saturday definitely seemed to have stirred up strong emotions. My error in judgment was in ignoring the KKK's attempts and its first rally on the north side of Sevierville. Because no more than three dozen people attended that rally, I wrongly assumed that by not acknowledging them, that the entire episode would fade away—a spectacularly poor and naive determination on my part.

Within two weeks, the KKK had applied for and received a permit to hold a Saturday night rally on the courthouse square in downtown Sevierville. This time, we not only acknowledged their actions, but editorialized against their effort, saying that we didn't need "rabble-rousing outsiders" intruding into Sevier County's business. The words sounded familiar, but the cause was reversed, as racial tensions in Mississippi were afire at that very same time.

"An open letter about the KKK
AN EDITORIAL

Sevierville continues to be invaded by the hate-spreading, sheet-shrouded members of the Ku Klux Klan. Many responsible members of our community were sickened by the sight of a Klan rally held at the courthouse Saturday night. Nearly every one of the Klansmen and spectators were from out of town . . . mostly from Blount County, some from Knox County.

In addition to the regular robes, some half a dozen Klansmen were dressed in blue uniforms, with crash helmets and combat boots, and carrying clubs attached to their belts. They were apparently there to "keep order." This, too, was a sickening [sight] in our hometown.

We feel this is a problem worthy of concern by all responsible citizens. It would be nice to be able to look the other way and hope the problem would disappear. This is something that could affect the reputation of our town, the economy of our town, and possibly the morals of the community.

We feel the time has come for us to make our We confidently feel the vast majority of our citizens are in direct opposition to everything the KKK stands for, and feelings known. You can write, call, or see your city councilman, city policemen, or anyone in authority and let them know how you stand. We should be united.

We are assured that our governmental authorities are not in sympathy with the KKK and as this newspaper has stated before, we feel that our local citizens can handle any legal action that will be taken when laws are broken or problems we might have in our town. It looks like the KKK is becoming one of those problems.

The KKK should stay home and stay away from decent people who don't wish to have their lives contaminated with hate.

BR

On the day of the rally, the KKK had their military police–like minions patrolling the streets, handing out leaflets promoting the rally (somebody else obviously did accept their business). The patrollers were an imposing sight unless, as one friend put it, you tried to engage them in a conversation. One wag noted: "None of them were even close to being threatened by a triple-digit IQ." The head of the local volunteer fire department called and said if they lit a cross at the rally, "the cross and a lot of hooded leaders" were going to be thoroughly doused. Curiosity and a strange kind of excitement began to build.

My neighbor, friend, and political confidante, Johnny Waters drove us to the event. We decided to stand in the back, near a beautiful oak tree, and just observe. The stage looked sturdy, and if not for what they represented, the leaders' robes might have been considered festive. We guessed that about half the crowd were from out-of-town; the other 50 or so attendees were locals.

The program began harmlessly enough. But, when Robert Shelton, the Imperial Wizard of the United Klans of America (Shelton hailed from Tuscaloosa) stood up, I was taken aback when he began his remarks by attacking our newspapers and ranting against me personally. I remained calm until Shelton made the mistake of saying, "He doesn't know what's going on," in reference to me. There are few more insulting comments that one could make about a newsman; my blood immediately began boiling.

Anyone who knows me now, or knew me then, knows that I'm a fairly laid-back guy, not prone to impetuous actions or statements. But, I stepped right out of character that night.

"Do *you* know what's going on?" I bellowed from the back of the crowd. During the stunned silence which followed, one of the MP-dressed, helmet-wearing, night-stick-carrying agitators made his way over to where I stood and said, "Hold it down, buddy!"

At that point, my fuse blew. I exploded, and started yelling, "Who are you to tell me anything in my own courthouse square?"

"Show me your credentials," I shouted.

Thank goodness my words appeared to catch him off guard, because he was considerably larger than me. There was human electricity crackling in the air when a small, wiry local, who was well-known for enjoying Saturday nights with spirits and fast fists, yelled in my direction, "You get that'un over there, and I'll take those two, Bo." His supportiveness and willingness to go at it on my behalf made me laugh. I heeded the encouragement of my calm, collected neighbor, who said it was time to go. It was possibly some of the finest advice I'd ever received and taken.

I don't know what transpired in the square after that, but I was told that things quickly dissipated.

At least until 2 a.m. that morning. My family was awakened by the sound of rocks hitting the front window of our house, and the glow of a burning cross ablaze in the front yard.

Thus began several weeks of nefarious activity, which included threatening phone calls. These were usually made in my absence, but the information conveyed was always the same: the caller either said I would not make it home that night, or asked if my wife knew where I was and with whom. After, and including the cross burning, we made it a ritual to report everything that happened to the police. As it became more routine, the effects of the harassment became less frightening and more annoying..

Things were slowing down a bit, but the crowning blow came when the Sevier County Ministerial Association, led by Baptist home missionary Bill Atchley, passed a unanimous resolution denouncing the KKK and supporting the Board of Education and our newspapers. That group's action was dutifully reported on our front pages and diffused any remaining steam which the KKK had in Sevier County.

"Ministers Take Stand Against KKK Activities"

"TO THE CITIZENS OF SEVIER COUNTY:

The members of the Sevier County Interdenominational Ministerial Association who were present at the June meeting Wednesday wish to express publicly their strong disapproval of the recent presence of and the tactics employed by the Ku Klux Klan.

We call upon all citizens of the county who profess to be Christian servants to join us in making it known that the KKK is not welcome here. We have reasons to believe that this organization might bring turmoil and disorder to a community that has handled its social affairs well and has done so without outside interference.

We deplore the very presence of the KKK and are requesting that our law enforcement officers and other county and city officials do all in their power to stop the activities of this group in Sevierville and Sevier County.

Furthermore, we call upon all citizens to join together in this effort to stop KKK activities amongst us.

The Sevier County
Interdenominational Ministerial Association

At least, I thought the Klan hubbub was over until several months later. After I had left for a new job in Atlanta, I was reminded about letting my hair grow and the visit from the two "interns." My story wasn't included in the *Life* exposé, as it was fairly tame in comparison to the scars that the *Life* magazine writer showed me from his undercover experiences with the KKK. However, we bonded that day and mutually confessed to the outright prejudice which we both held against the KKK.....regardless of hairstyle.

Clockwise left to right: Top left: Johnny Waters, Co-chairman, was appointed to the Appalachian Regional Commission by President Richard Nixon. *Photo courtesy of Cyndy Waters.* R: Gene Hickey. *Photo courtesy of Sally Hickey.* Bottom: Sevierville Chamber of Commerce Founding Board of Directors, 1963: L-R (seated) Lyle McNabb, Hugh Trotter, Ross Summitt; (standing) Jimmie Temple, Bo Roberts, E.W. "Cap" Paine, Dr. John Hickey, Judge Ray Reagan, Charlie Bell. Temple and Reagan were two of my "heroes." *Photo courtesy of Carroll McMahan, Sevierville Chamber of Commerce.*

Bill Postlewaite, the owner and publisher of the *Gatlinburg Press* and the *Sevier County News-Record*. *Photo courtesy of the Postlewaite family.*

The Roberts and Waters kids in Sevierville: L-R Sam Roberts, Andy Roberts, Johnny B. Waters, Mark Roberts and Cyndy Waters aka "Little Momma." *Photo courtesy of Cyndy Waters.*

3

....

FINDING OUT
WHAT YOU DO AND DON'T
WANT TO DO

....

Round Peg in a Square Hole

After nearly four years in the newspaper business in Sevier County, despite the remarkable people and the extraordinary business deal that Bill Postlewaite had put together for me, when I was approached by a major national company about my interest in a potential new position, I confirmed my interest.

I had to admit to myself that my deal with Postlewaite meant that I would be doing the same thing for the next 6–10 years. As interesting and challenging as that was, it was still doing pretty much the same thing in different ways. I had had offers before, from the *Knoxville News-Sentinel* and the *Chattanooga Times*, but they couldn't pay me as much as I was making at the Mountain Press, due to their union agreements. As a guy with a young family and not much of a nest egg, I really couldn't afford the opportunity to earn daily newspaper experience.

The company that approached me was Bell South, part of the national monopoly, AT&T Corporation. The position they offered was in marketing and advertising, working from the Bell South headquarters in Atlanta. It sounded interesting, and the proposed salary was a sizable jump for a guy just four years out of college. During our discussions, I recall that the recruiter commented that they normally hired folks who were just out of college, rather than offering more substantial salaries to qualified, seasoned prospects.

In any event, I was intrigued, talked it over with my family, and decided to accept the offer and make the change. As agonizing as it was to share my decision with Mr. Postlewaite, I sensed that he had suspected that this day might arrive eventually, despite his most generous plan.

So, off to Atlanta we went. I was excited about the opportunity with no fear of the unknowns. We bought a house in the suburbs of Atlanta, in Decatur, and by the end of the first week, I'd joined a carpool with three other guys who also worked downtown in the Hurt Building, one of America's first skyscrapers. Wow, this was big city stuff compared to Sevier County, and to my hometown of Harriman.

After orientation, my assignment was to develop all of what was called the "non-paid" advertising program. In those days, people primarily went to their local Bell South office to pay their phone bills. The advertising I was in charge of developing included the signs that customers saw when they came into the office, promoting various company products and options. It also included the signage on the sides of the thousands of Bell South trucks that traveled our nine-state territory, the flyers included in the mail with phone bills, and other documents.

I was a little out of my lane, but with the help of a full-time artist and junior staff members, we created a plan that passed muster. After about four months of preparation, I presented it to the Bell South Board of Directors, who seemed very receptive—or, at least, that was the feedback from my boss, which pleased him immensely.

I figuratively wiped my hands and eagerly asked, "Okay, what's next?" Well, not much, as it turned out. Thus began my realization, unnoticed at the time, of what I did not want to do with my life. I had several months to tweak, and possibly present a new plan. In the meantime, I could assist my boss, who was chairman of the National Cancer Society drive in his suburban county with his tasks, and lend a hand on other various outreach projects that had the company's support. There was nothing wrong with any of that, and, I say to this day, that Bell South was a stellar company. However, my mind kept drifting back to the recruiter musing ......"Hmmm, well, we usually hire people right out of college."

I had been "spoiled" early in my career by having been virtually on my own, never working to a clock, spending whatever time it took to get a job done, loving deadlines, and loathing any error I made, while feeling satisfaction with any accolades that came my way.

After less than 11 months on the job, in a word, I was bored. As a way of keeping in touch, I had sent one of my articles to my former Journalism Dean at UT. In his reply, he had sent a note saying, "Here's what you should be doing." A copy of the job description for the editor of the UT System news bureau was enclosed. I had worked with, and for, the leadership there during my student days. I leapt at the opportunity. I sped to Knoxville for an interview that very weekend, accepted the job, and sold our house on Monday morning (one of my carpool mates' father was a realtor) before I informed my boss about my imminent departure. I tried to hide my excitement as I delivered the news while offering whatever notice was customary.

He was shocked—they simply were not accustomed to having people leave the company. I could certainly understand why. With a path to regular promotions and access to the kind of stock options that made long-time employees wealthy, "jumping ship" just didn't happen that often. Again, while it was an outstanding company, I quickly discovered that I was not a good fit there. Little did I know then that my next move would lead to politics, presidents, and a world stage.

4

BACK TO UT

My official title was editor of the news bureau. I oversaw UT publications and press releases for media throughout the state. My area of responsibility included the main campus in Knoxville, UT-Martin, and the medical units at UT-Memphis (this was prior to Chattanooga joining the UT system). I worked for people in public relations whom I had gotten to know well as a student, such as Julian Harriss and Neal O'Steen. As with Sevier County, I dug right in and began developing contacts for stories. I think I did a good job; we set some records with the number of stories generated and publications produced. Of course, the internet didn't exist then. We saw the fruits of our labors each week when we received our package of clippings, which was usually overflowing with stories cut directly from the publications in which they had appeared. This was a valuable service operated as part of the state press association.

I wrote stories and had people writing for me, as well. We touted the university's accomplishments, its research results, and grants awarded. Once, the Census Bureau released a report through UT about population updates. With some students assisting, we did a story about each county and the impact of their specific population change. The resulting coverage ran in nearly every one of the state's more than

94 counties. As an editor in Sevier County, I know when I received a press release about something happening in our county, I gave it special consideration and placement.

I was enjoying my work and I felt so at home.

We'd bought a house in the suburbs, and our kids were starting school. Everything felt comfortable. A few months in, my boss, Julian, talked to me about who I might support for governor. I told him I hadn't completely decided, but was considering supporting Gov. Ellington's re-election bid. I had met him a few times, both through my newspaper work, and at the annual "State of the State" speech, hosted by the Tennessee Press Association. I agreed with Ellington on many issues. Now I learned that the governor wanted to talk to me about a job.

First, let me give some background about the relationship between the state university system and state government. At the time, Andy Holt, UT president, was the first non-agricultural president ever appointed. He was a progressive, yet homespun man; he made more money giving speeches around the country with his great sense of humor than he ever did as university president. Few people were ever aware that Holt donated the money he earned making speeches for scholarships.

Working with then-Governor Clement, they decided to professional-ize some elements of state government. For example, based on UT's recommendation, the governor had appointed Ed Boling as the first professional budget director (this role later became the state Commissioner of Finance and Administration). Another recent graduate, Bill Snodgrass, was tapped to serve as comptroller of the Treasury. There was a productive relationship, with the state government looking to the university system for professional help.

Gov. Ellington's opponent, John Jay Hooker, Jr., was a young political gadfly with the strong backing of the *Nashville Tennessean*. Ellington realized that Hooker—a volatile, talented lawyer and fantastic public speaker—and his campaign were eating his lunch, so to speak, with research and tactics. So Ellington called Andy Holt and asked for help. They recommended me.

I went to meet the governor for an interview. He was about my father's age, and we hit it off. I called him "Governor" as he had previously served as governor (at that time Tennessee governors were prohibited from serving consecutive terms). He kept referring to me as "Dr. Bo"—he thought everyone from UT had a Ph.D. since two other men in the university–state pipeline, Ed Boling and Joe Johnson, had earned their doctorates at Peabody. I politely corrected him. I had gone into our first meeting with this mindset: If the governor said, "I'll give you the job, and if we win, I'll give you this other job," I might not have accepted it. I found out later that Ellington felt the same way. If I'd only agreed to take the job on the condition of receiving something more as the result of a winning campaign, he confided that he would not have hired me. It was good to be on the same wavelength.

Gov. Ellington officially offered me the position. My assignment was researching issues and writing speeches. I did not tell him that I'd never written a speech for somebody else, nor did I tell him that I'd never been involved in a campaign at the gubernatorial level. Funnily enough, I had no hesitation whatsoever about the skill set needed for the job. I was confident in my natural ability to communicate.

After less than a year, I took a leave of absence from the UT News Bureau to join the governor's re-election bid. The university administrators had indicated that they would be happy to have me back following the campaign. There was an inherent risk, though. If Ellington had been unsuccessful, I don't believe that the winning candidate would have been too keen on my returning to a high-profile position at a state-funded institution.

But, I rolled the dice and headed west to Nashville.

5

·················

YOUNGEST GOVERNOR'S ASSISTANT

··

The Bitter Campaign

I'd transitioned from the youngest editor to the youngest governor's assistant. The campaign headquarters were located in a Nashville hotel, so it made sense for me to stay in a room near the office. I existed on room service, worked crazy hours, and traveled with the campaign. With access to people in government, including both the Clement and Ellington administrations, the focus of my research was to assess what was going on in state government, and develop positions based on the issues.

At that time, television was a nascent medium, and campaigns were driven mostly by campaign rallies and speeches given in different town squares. For example, one of the traditions at that time was that the candidates would deliver their platform speech at some point during the campaign. It was their opportunity to inform voters of their positions and address issues. Considered *the* major speech, it was the center point from which everything radiated. Prior to that pivotal moment, the candidate road-tested various position parts, depending upon the audience. For example, business policies might be first presented to a business-oriented audience. While tv stations covered campaign events and we purchased television advertising, there was no substitute for shaking hands at rallies in town squares packed with voters. These appearances comprised the bulk of campaign activity.

Spanning April through August (which seemed like a year), campaigning comprised the most intense work I'd ever done. I went home to Knoxville only two or three weekends during those months; I hardly saw my family at all. I remember saying that the best thing about campaigns was that they were eventually over, though it seemed endless. Also, the measure of how well one did the job was super simple: Did you win or did you lose?

Gov. Ellington was facing a different kind of election this time, as Tennessee's political system only required a plurality to win. There were no runoffs in either the primary or the general election. When he had been elected eight years before, there had been three dominant candidates and a handful of also-rans. In that election (1958), he received just 213,415 votes (31.14 %) out of the more than 684,000 cast; so, while Ellington didn't receive a majority, he garnered more than either of his two main challengers. In contrast, this campaign (1966) was a straight up, one-on-one, head-to-head contest. The brash, flamboyant John Jay Hooker was supported by the liberal *Tennessean* while we had the endorsement of the *Nashville Banner*, a far more moderate, traditional paper.

It was an extremely intense, very bitter campaign. In terms of personal style, the two men were poles apart. Candidate Hooker was, at age 36, dashing, dapper, and dandy, while the 59-year-old former governor was a conventional, conservative Democrat in a standard, classically cut suit. Though the two were never outright enemies, they were, by any assessment, from opposite ends of every spectrum. Both had hired a cadre of seasoned political warriors from previous campaigns, so there was continuity, mainly among the battle-hardened professionals on staff.

As a journalist, I was astonished by the press coverage. The "news" stories which appeared in the *Tennessean* would make me feel glum and depressed until the early editions of the *Banner* appeared later in the morning. The *Banner's* perspective, favoring Ellington, of course, raised our spirits right back up, infusing us with fresh energy. For example, if an Ellington rally in Columbia (in Middle Tennessee's Maury County) drew huge crowds of 25,000 spectators, the *Tennessean* would print that 7,000–8,000 people had attended, while the *Banner* would peg the number at 20,000–30,000. Actual attendance was probably between 15,000 and 18,000 spectators, but one couldn't accurately determine a real number by the reporting. The overly partisan press coverage truly shocked me because I hadn't lived in Nashville. I'd certainly been exposed to newspapers fighting for dominance in Knoxville, but those turf wars were child's play compared to the cat-scratching that went on in the state's capital.

One anecdotal event that occurred was this: I, along with a few staffers and some media members were having drinks prior to one of Gov. Ellington's major speeches, when a fellow reporter asked Ken Morrell, who was the *Nashville Banner's* senior political reporter, if he considered himself to be an objective reporter. Morrell, who a few years later would be named editor of the *Banner*, replied: "I sure do. I have one objective and that is to get Buford Ellington elected governor!" Morrell had clearly not misunderstood his marching orders from the *Banner's* publisher.

So, this political battle had been framed as the young liberal versus the "leapfrog government," which Ellington represented. Frank Clement had served the final two-year gubernatorial term and the first four-year term (1952 through 1958), after Tennesseans voted to change the state constitution to permit four-year terms; however, a governor was still unable to succeed himself. By the time Gov. Ellington, Clement's former campaign manager and former state Commissioner of Agriculture, ran and won the second four-year term, their cumulative years in office was a decade. With another term each for both men, the state Democratic party held the state's top office for 18 years.

With that much political history, I was already fairly well aware of Gov. Ellington's previous positions on the issues. During his first term, eight years prior, one of his platform lines was, "I'm a segregationist; an old-fashioned segregationist." That was a mammoth statement to repudiate and overcome. Attempting to address and contain the effects of that particular position, became the basis of one of the most sensitive speeches I'd ever written (then or now). At the time, H. T. Lockard (a Black man and top campaign official) and I had become buddies. I first met the Memphis lawyer and political leader in 1966. Because the former governor was well-known as a staunch segregationist, it took guts as big as the Mississippi River was wide for Lockard to become one of the campaign's top managers. Predictably, he suffered a barrage of criticism for that decision.

I went to Lockard and asked where we should start, what we should say—what would have meaning for him? His profound sentiment was this: "Times change. Wise men change with the times."

We used Lockard's quote as the foundation from which to address the concerns of Black voters, and we did receive a lot of support. It was quite momentous to overcome not just segregation but, especially, the three words: "old-fashioned segregationist." Gov. Ellington had obviously undergone a change of heart. Over the years, he had become close friends and allies with President Lyndon Johnson. He led the charge on Johnson's behalf in "selling" the landmark Civil Rights Act to Southern governors, and served as Johnson's Director of the Office of Emergency Planning.

Gov. Ellington first used the phrase: "Times change.....Wise men change with the times" at a campaign platform speech in Jackson, about 85 miles east of Memphis.

I don't recall many of the words I wrote in that section, which followed his opening statement, because the resonance of those first eight words continued to ring in my head for years afterward. In fact, almost no one remembered the words which followed. The impact of those two sentences was so searing, so gripping, so pointed, and so true, that they genuinely said all that needed to be said. The governor totally embraced Lockard's approach and reinforced his commitment that times had changed. Ellington delivered the line (we thought) with passion and conviction on that warm, energy-filled night in Jackson.

He further amplified that point and took a position on not increasing sales tax because Gov. Clement had run as a progressive and raised taxes. Ellington's theme was, "A man of his word." Throughout the speech, I sprinkled in another significant phrase for him to use whenever he made an emphatic point. He would stop and say, "And, on this, I give you my word," to thunderous applause. Of course, I kept thinking that if I were on the other side, I'd say, "Are these the only things you give your word on?" But we managed to survive. Apparently, I did a worthy job, because some of the older politicos I've counseled with were very complimentary to the governor and me on the job he did. The positions he took ended up winning. The final vote was 413,950 to 360,105. Ellington won by an eight-point margin. And, as we all know, winning is the best position of all.

Transitions—In, Out, Back

I didn't know what I would do after the campaign. My former PR boss at UT, Julian Harriss, thought I'd be back. However, Joe Johnson, who would be a colleague of mine when he was the vice president at the university (and later president) of UT, said in a meeting with then-president Andy Holt and others, "If Bo Roberts does the job I think he'll do in Nashville and Gov. Ellington wins, he won't be back."

I didn't have expectations either way. But Gov. Ellington let it be known right afterward that he wanted me as part of his administration. Many in the campaign were joining outgoing-Gov. Clement's campaign for the U.S. Senate. His opponent was my friend, Howard Baker. Gov. Clement was not an enemy; he was a friend, too, but I didn't know him that well. With so many from Gov. Ellington's campaign moving over to assist with Clement's senatorial campaign, Ellington asked me if I wanted to do the same? I explained to him that I had nothing against Gov. Clement, but said that I would feel very uncomfortable working against Baker. I also pointed out that his campaign manager was another close friend. The governor said that wasn't a problem and asked me to oversee the transition, with the intention that I would be part of his administration, beginning with his inauguration in January of 1967.

We sold our house in Knoxville and moved to Nashville. I knew I would be there for at least four years. It was the experience of a lifetime.

The transition office was set up at the National Guard Armory. I had a spacious office with a desk that seemed as big as an aircraft carrier. I gathered information about state departments and who I'd need to interview for the cabinet. Some National Guard officers worked in the armory, and as a former buck sergeant, I was impressed by the military brass. I mentioned as much to Governor-elect Ellington, and he said, "In four years, they won't know your name." He was right. Political power constantly shifts, and today's leader might be tomorrow's loser. That was the first of many political lessons I learned under Gov. Ellington, who was accustomed to the vagaries of being an officeholder. It had a leavening effect on me. I remained level-headed amidst the heady atmosphere.

Shifting Legislative Winds

A governor's cabinet meetings were seldom (if ever) disturbed, but this one got them stirring.

It was a few days before the inauguration of newly re-elected Gov. Ellington, and his staff and cabinet appointments were complete. His appointees were meeting in the spacious living room of his private Glen Leven residence in Nashville. We had been reviewing the basics of daily operations and procedures when the call came. One of our legislative leaders telephoned to say that the state's General Assembly, just beginning its Monday afternoon session, was about to consider a resolution calling for annual sessions.

This was heresy; the governor hadn't been consulted. How dare the legislature consider such a bold move to change things so radically? The governor immediately sprang into action. Every cabinet and staff member with experience working with the legislature was dispatched to the capitol to "put a stop to all this."

Out they marched with their orders, looking determined and resolved. The Governor's "army" included former House Speaker Dick Barry, Treasurer Charlie Worley (a former House member), powerful Commissioner of Education Howard Warf, campaign manager and former State Senator Bob Taylor, and others.

As a newcomer to state government, I had not yet had the pleasure or the pain of working with the state legislature. Those with a similar lack of direct experience remained with the governor and me.

While waiting, I reflected on the significance. Tennessee was known as a strong governor state, meaning that the governor pretty much ruled and the legislature complied with his wishes. The "biennial" legislature was just that.....it met every other year. The just convened 85th General Assembly was trying to change that tradition.

I had heard the budget stories about Gov. Ellington's first term: When he submitted his budget, it was sent "upstairs" to the legislature and returned for his signature in less time than it usually took for lunch. The massive bill had passed all committees and both houses in a scant 45 minutes.

There had been a major stir on legislative independence during Gov. Frank Clement's last term (Clement was set to leave office after three separate terms and a total of 10 years as the state's chief executive). The state senate had had the audacity to want to elect its own speaker rather than the one the governor had handpicked. The uproar had been one of the major news stories two years earlier. The result had produced a crack in the powerful dam that was the governor's stronghold. Frank Gorrell was elected speaker and thus became Lieutenant Governor. It had been a significant coup for our campaign when Lt. Gov. Gorrell endorsed Gov. Ellington (but that's another story).

After about two hours, Ellington's warriors returned. Their collective gait was slow; they trudged in with shoulders slumped. No actual blood graced their foreheads, but there might as well have been. Dick Barry had the unenviable task of reporting to the governor-elect that the legislature was moving towards annual sessions. When individually polled, the somber nods and replies confirmed that the issue had virtually been decided.

All eyes in the room were on Gov. Ellington as he absorbed the news. During the long pause, you could almost see Ellington's mind working. Finally, he said, "Folks, let's get in touch with our floor leaders (our legislative friends who sponsored and carried all administration bills and positions) and have them convey to their colleagues that we're looking forward to working with them."

For better or worse, the shift toward legislative independence had already begun.

When Mere Presence Made a Difference

I first learned how deafening silence truly could be while in the governor's conference room at the Tennessee State Capitol more than 50 years ago.

The state's highway commissioner had just noted the main reason (in his opinion) that an interstate route was selected to be located in downtown Nashville, "You know, just a bunch of n-----s live down there."

The extraordinary silence that followed the commissioner's comment could be traced to the presence of one man, the first African-American ever appointed to a cabinet-level position in Tennessee's history. As the governor's administrative assistant, H. T. Lockard was not there as a token, nor did he seem to have ambitions toward being a hero. Yet, his presence heralded a new day, one in which traditional southern policy would be made differently.

Following the brutal, but victorious campaign, Lockard and I were two of the first four appointments to Governor-elect Ellington's cabinet-level staff. Our offices were next to each other on the first floor of the Capitol building, so we saw each other daily. We both had to adjust to the farm upbringing of our boss, who started every work day with a 7 a.m. staff meeting. During this two-hour period, various commissioners would appear in order to discuss their issues and problems, air their grievances, or review opportunities with the governor and his staff.

It was at one of those meetings that the highway commissioner reported on a looming lawsuit about the interstate program in Nashville. The commissioner, who was a career state employee and a good man, was stating what had been customary, the culture, and the historical practice of the times. The silence only lasted a few seconds but it was deafening, when the commissioner sheepishly looked up at Lockard and mumbled, "Well, you know what I mean."

Lockard gave no reply. He just smiled as he steadily held the Commissioner's gaze. Finally, the Governor said, "Charlie, things aren't like they used to be."

At that moment, I felt the full impact of the magnitude of presence. Nothing replaces either being at the table or being in the room. It is what tips the scales; changes the balance. Never again would I discount so-called "token" appointments. On that day, H. T. Lockard's presence set the Volunteer State on a more enlightened, more progressive course. Though this quiet, thoughtful man, who would later be appointed as a Criminal Court judge in Shelby County, didn't come to Nashville to be a champion, he became the kind of unsung, uncelebrated hero that one doesn't hear much about. Even time doesn't change that.

Expensive "Pork"

Anyone who knows UT knows that if you travel on I-40 through Knoxville, the 17th Street exit leads to the Knoxville campus. At the time that I was working in the governor's office, there was no indication, no sign. I called the Commissioner of Highways to try to understand this oversight. He and his chief of staff met with me in the governor's office, where I inquired about getting a UT sign on the interstate exit. He looked into it, came back, and said that the Federal Bureau of Public Roads wouldn't allow it.

That summer, I was on vacation with my family, traveling through Kentucky, Ohio, Virginia, and back through North Carolina. With my Polaroid camera, I took pictures in these states of various exit signs which read: *Western Kentucky University* or the *University of Virginia*. I mounted all of the photos on a poster board and asked the Bureau of Highways leadership to drop by. I showed them my display and asked, "Do Kentucky, Virginia and Ohio all have the same Bureau of Public Roads that we work with?" They sheepishly admitted that they did.. I asked them to get the UT sign in process.

A few weeks later, they returned and said, well, we would need to install signs for *all* state universities, and that the projected cost was $3 million (1967 dollars). Somewhat to their surprise, I said, "Fine." We got it done. That's one of the favors I did for UT. I kiddingly tell the few people who know about this that if you're driving down the interstate in Tennessee and see a sign for a university campus, give me either the credit or blame.

Another (less expensive) sign story is that there were no road signs in Nashville indicating the location of our historic State Capitol building; not from interstates 65, or 40, or 24. As there is only one state capital, I knew that we wouldn't have to be concerned about any additional signage. It still took into the waning months of Ellington's four-year term to get that capital sign installed. Bureaucracy has a way of paying you back.

Shaking Up and Reshaping Tennessee Higher Education

He taught me the definition of "sidle up" and how a small, reserved man could so completely dominate a profession where even college presidents were visibly unnerved when they talked about him.

"He" was Howard Warf, who had been reappointed as Commissioner of Education by Gov. Buford Ellington following his re-election to a second term in 1966. As the young Turk, named as Ellington's top policy assistant, I was directed by the governor to prioritize the re-organization of higher education in Tennessee. Part of the reason I was given the assignment was that I joined the Ellington campaign on leave of absence from the University of Tennessee, which made me the higher education guru (or like most other things he assigned to me, I think he thought or hoped I would find a way to figure it out).

But, back to Warf. The diminutive, soft-spoken man came to the state government from Lewis County (where Meriwether Lewis was buried in 1809) in Middle Tennessee. From his home in the county seat of Hohenwald, Warf ruled like a king; whomever he supported for governor generally received about two-thirds of the vote. At the time that he was appointed Commissioner of Education by Gov. Frank Clement, the Tennessee Department of Education had jurisdiction over the state's entire public education system with the exception of the University of Tennessee. "Entire" included ruling kindergarten through 12th grade, the burgeoning community college system, and all six "regional" colleges (East Tennessee State, Middle Tennessee State, Austin Peay, Tennessee Tech, Tennessee State, and Memphis State).

And "rule" was the operative word for Warf. No major decisions or appointments were made without his express approval. He maintained his power by demanding loyalty and kept the legislature at bay with just enough consultation and special favors when needed. Watching him work the halls in the Capitol offered a masterful lesson in political theater. It was also where I saw, firsthand, what it meant to "sidle up" to someone. One might be in deep conversation with someone when the Commissioner of Education would appear, waiting to talk about a point of interest (always his point, of course).

None of this is to say he was either an evil person or an ineffective administrator, but, in the view of most of the six college presidents in Tennessee, he clearly had a K-12 bias (there were more K-12 teachers and families than were professors, more K-12 students, and more votes). Dr. Cecil "Sonny" Humphreys, then president of Memphis State University, would complain that although he was heading the second largest institution in the state, Memphis State issues received a paltry 10–15 minutes of consideration during the two-day quarterly meetings of the Board of Education.

On the campaign trail, Gov. Ellington heard, privately, from the college presidents, time and again, that change was desperately needed. He committed to instituting change, if elected. That's where I came in. At Ellington's direction, I met with UT Vice President Ed Boling (Ellington's trusted Commissioner of Finance and Administration during his first term, who would become president of UT four years later) and Middle Tennessee State University President Quill Cope (a respected educator and personal friend of the Ellingtons). From that meeting, the concept was developed for a new Board of Regents for the six colleges and universities and a coordinating board to oversee the two systems of higher education.

The legislation was drafted to create the Tennessee Higher Education Commission (THEC) as the coordinating board, giving it powers such as location selection for the next seven community colleges. THEC's main charge was to develop a funding formula for higher education and to approve or disapprove new programs in order to avoid duplication among, and between, colleges and systems.

The companion piece of legislation was the creation of the Tennessee Board of Regents (TBR), which would be the governing board for the six universities and the (then) two community colleges. Because UT had a president of its system and chancellors at its campuses (then Martin and Memphis), the Regents' system was set up to have a chancellor-in-charge with the campuses having presidents. The central purpose was that it would be an independent board, totally separate from the Board of Education and, more importantly, free from the clutches of Warf (though the Commissioner of Education would be an ex-officio member of the Board).

With the draft legislation in hand, it was time to sell it. My first assignment was to conduct clandestine meetings with some of the college presidents to brief them, solicit their input and, hopefully, gain their support. It seemed ludicrous that the mission was so hush-hush, kept secret from the man the governor had appointed as his commissioner. But, that's how it had to be, apparently, so I didn't waste any time questioning the process; I just attempted to carry it out.

Obviously, MTSU President Cope was supportive since he had assisted in drafting the legislation. I remember when we went over things with Gov. Ellington, he kept asking, "Quill, are you OK with this?" and "Does this do the job?" Dr. Cope assured him that it was fine and would provide him and his colleagues with freedom and breathing room. Sadly, Dr. Cope didn't live to see his creation implemented as he passed away before its implementation. Fittingly, though, his grandson, Murfreesboro attorney E. Evan Cope, continued the storied family education legacy when he became chairman of Tennessee's Higher Education Commission in 2015.

My next visit was with Dr. D. P. Culp at East Tennessee State University in Johnson City. I was scheduled to fly in on the governor's plane at night and meet with President Culp early the next morning. Unbeknownst to me, my secretary had trouble securing a room at the Holiday Inn, so she imperiously declared, "This is for the governor's office. Bo Roberts is coming on a special mission for the governor." When the pilots and I arrived at the hotel that evening, the first thing we spotted was the gigantic marquee, which read:

WELCOME BO ROBERTS
GOVERNOR'S OFFICE

The trip was no longer a secret. Suffice it to say, this prompted some changes in the way we did things in my office. I chuckled later, but it wasn't a laughing matter when I met with Dr. Culp. He was gracious, but uneasy. He seemed slightly confused as to why such a young person had been sent to see him. In any event, we dutifully reviewed the proposed plan. While indicating that he was fully in favor of the reorganization, Culp made it crystal clear that he couldn't openly support it until he was confident that it would be passed by the legislature. That's when I fully understood the depth and severity of anxiety that Warf engendered. These professional educators were far more apprehensive about the retribution that would be extracted by Warf as retaliation for their complicity, than they were about the extraordinary possibilities that would result from the potential outcome. I was sitting in the office of the person who "was" ETSU; Culp had nurtured this institution, giving it everything he had, for nearly two decades. And, yet, he was leery beyond comprehension of a person who had never spent one single day in charge of a comparable entity. It was beyond mind-blowing. Seeing Culp's reaction on that frigid January day spurred me on like a bone-weary horse galloping wide open toward its barn. I was resolute: we *would* win this one.

Visit no. 3 was to Dr. Joe Morgan, president of Austin Peay State University in Clarksville. Located on Tennessee's northern border near Fort Campbell, Kentucky, APSU was another school guided by a dedicated champion. Morgan was a legend in higher education circles, having accomplished more with limited resources than could possibly be expected. The epitome of gentility, this educator's reaction to the plan mirrored Dr. Culp's. Morgan felt that the state desperately needed the change, but had no interest in being lured in with the possibility unless our proposal had the wings to fly. I assured him that the governor was fully committed to the legislation and that we were going to see it through.

We then flew to Memphis to meet with Dr. Humphreys at Memphis State. A strapping man who had been urged by many to run for governor, President Humphreys didn't seem as uneasy as his fellow colleagues (I didn't know at the time that he would be departing to take another position in a few short months). Dr. Humphreys shared many stories about the iron-fisted Warf, and the games the presidents' played in attempting to circumvent the "Warf system." It was truly time for a new way of doing business.

My colleague, H. T. Lockard, was assigned to handle this matter with the president of Tennessee State University (as one Black man to another). My visit to Tennessee Tech University (TTU) was reserved until just one day before the plan's announcement. This allowed time for the chief legislative executive assistant, Dick Barry (former speaker of the House from Lexington, Tennessee), to brief the state's legislative leaders. Tennessee Tech was last on the list because its President, Everett Derryberry, was known far-and-wide as Warf's staunchest ally. He was fiercely loyal to TTU (particularly its engineering school). He managed the university in the same unyielding fashion that Warf ran the Department of Education. Derryberry was equally in step with Warf, plus he had the ability to deliver the Upper Cumberland legislators on key votes, which meant that he was generously rewarded when the higher ed dollars were apportioned. As I had predicted, my visit to TTU with Dr. Derryberry was an exercise in futility—he was not in favor of the change, felt that the plan had no chance of succeeding; and was perfectly happy with the status quo.

I also knew that he could be counted on to phone Warf immediately upon my departure with all of the details. Much to my surprise, I later became friends with the dynamic, portly Derryberry, who was seen as a formidable operative in both the annals of higher education and on the Tennessee political scene.

That afternoon the governor summoned Commissioner Warf to his office, so that we could apprise him of the plan. Warf did his dead level best to change the governor's mind, but deduced that Ellington was adamant. Warf quickly assessed that this was not a battle he would win that day. And, I say "battle" because for Warf (no political neophyte he), this war wasn't over by a long shot. In fact, Dick Barry continued to get word from our legislative leaders that Warf was speaking to legislators in an effort to sabotage the Governor's legislation. Numerous times during that session, an ordinarily calm Barry, red-faced with anger, would arrange for the two of us, along with the governor, to meet with Commissioner Warf. On at least five occasions, the governor admonished Warf with the words: "Howard, either get this straightened out, or I will fire you today!" Somehow, we managed to outfox our wily, stubborn appointee in order to reorganize higher education in Tennessee.

If there were those who disagreed as to whether the two new boards made higher education better, they'll never convince me that things didn't improve dramatically once the changes were implemented. THEC either halted or slowed the proliferation of costly programs, undertook a professional review in recommending locations for new community colleges, and later, developed a funding formula based on a school's mission. Today, the Board of Regents has grown into the nation's sixth largest higher education system and, with the addition of the Technology Centers, now oversees more than 46 institutions. Was the system perfect? Nah, nothing is; but, it was a darn sight better than it had been.

(Post note: I consistently disagreed with Commissioner Warf more than any other individual that I worked with in the Ellington administration. We did, however, develop a grudging respect for one another in the end, and, eventually, a friendship that lasted a lifetime. His final triumphant harpoon? During the next administration, he persuaded the legislature to appoint him as a lifetime member of the Board of Regents. I had to laugh and tip my hat to him when I heard the news. I was not the least surprised that he had, once again, sidled up to the right legislator. In his later years, he "attended" meetings via conference call, never missing a meeting while he was alive.

Chattanooga Promise: Another Major Higher Education Move

During his second campaign, Gov. Ellington promised to bring public higher education to Chattanooga, the state's fourth largest city. The single higher education institution in Chattanooga was the privately owned and operated University of Chattanooga, a respected liberal arts college. At the same time we were working to reorganize the governance of public higher education, the governor directed me to work with the University of Tennessee to bring a campus to Chattanooga. While UT President Andy Holt initiated and led the effort, I attended meetings primarily to demonstrate Gov. Ellington's support. Early on in the process, we were approached by the U.C. hierarchy regarding a merger of their private institution with UT.

The school's leadership consisted primarily of wealthy, "old money" Chattanoogans, who funded and ran things exactly as they wished. But, they also realized that a public institution with lower tuition and overall costs would make for tough competition. From Dr. Holt's perspective, the resources of a substantial private foundation would provide additional "icing on the cake" (as he referred to private supplemental funding of a campus), and assist in advancing the timetable for opening a new campus.

Our discussions increased in intensity, before culminating in a meeting with the UC Foundation, chaired by William Brock, Jr. (his son, Bill Brock, III, would be elected to the U.S. Senate in 1970, after defeating Democrat Albert Gore, Sr.). As Brock outlined the plan, they were keen for the state to invest millions in upgrading and converting their campus to a substantial UT campus, while permitting their Foundation's Board of Directors to continue its unilateral oversight and direction. Dr. Holt and I listened closely to their pitch while passing several handwritten notes between us. Following their presentation, Holt said: "Well, Bo, I think these fine people have presented an interesting proposition that basically says they want to keep their private school. On behalf of UT and the state administration, we will not interfere with your operating your excellent institution. We will just be on our way and make plans to build a public UT campus. We thank you for your time."

And with that, we stood up, began gathering his papers, and prepared to leave. Mr. Brock, I remember clearly, turned several shades of red as he attempted to retain his composure. Finally, he said, with obvious discomfort: "Can we keep talking?" And then added: "Please."

Dr. Holt looked at me, I nodded and he said, "Of course, Mr. Chairman, if that's what you'd like." Thus began our serious, final negotiations, which ultimately led to the Foundation continuing with many of its original members on its Board. They would operate as a support system for a university that would be independently managed by the University of Tennessee staff and Board of Trustees, with reinforcement from the private Foundation and its fundraising prowess.

I don't want to imply that the local leaders weren't well-meaning people or that they had abnormally automatic intentions, it just made for a particularly laborious merger process. It all worked out, and with some bumps and hitches that were to be expected, the University of Tennessee Chattanooga (UTC) became a campus in which all of Southeast Tennessee could take pride.

"Mr. Hub": Lessons Learned from the Senator

His name was Herbert S. Walters, but everyone called him "Mr. Hub." Later, when he was appointed by Gov. Clement to fill out the remaining two years of the term of the late Senator Estes Kefauver of Memphis, people referred to him as "Senator Hub."

Mr. Hub hailed from Morristown. As the main contact in East Tennessee for the Democrats, Mr. Hub brokered deals with the Republicans on different candidates and issues. There was nothing nefarious about it, but that was their understanding and way of getting things done. I first got to know him when he was at UT as a long-time member of the Board of Trustees. He was extremely genteel and the epitome of a Southern political operative: understated, soft-spoken, yet extraordinarily persistent.

One of the things I handled in the governor's office was external meetings. Anytime that the governor was to leave the office, that invitation had to come through me for my approval, disapproval, or negotiation. Mr. Hub occasionally asked for something, and, with a man of his stature, you were just looking for ways to say yes. The only thing left to do was confirm dates and times. If I didn't get back to him soon enough, he would call and nicely say, "I just happened to be thinking about this and wanted to check in. So, if you need any more information from me, let me know." He was politely persistent; he almost always got what he wanted. And what he wanted was never a personal favor—it was something beneficial to his area or the entire state.

Once, Mr. Hub asked me and my friend, David Pack, the newly appointed attorney general, to be grand marshals in Morristown's Christmas parade. As stated, no one told Mr. Hub no. So, Pack and I, who at the time were the only East Tennessee residents in high political positions in Nashville, were on the reviewing stand a month before the inauguration in January, 1967. We reviewed the marching band and waved as they saluted us. Pack, who had also been Commissioner of Highways, leaned over and said, "Bo, it's okay to breathe a little of this. Just don't start inhaling." Another lesson learned. It was alright to enjoy a taste of the pomp and circumstance, but don't get addicted.

Hiring "Hands" Was Out

After we won the primary, which essentially meant we would win the election, we had a meeting on a farm in Middle Tennessee with all Ellington's county chairmen and contacts from those counties that would be used for recommendations and requests. One of the topics the governor-elect covered in that meeting was that we were continuing on the road toward the professionalization of state employees. There would be no more dismissing of the previous administration's employees to make room for hiring "friends." The longstanding practice had been that when a new governor came in, he jettisoned people he didn't care for and installed the people he wanted in state jobs in that county. Ellington stated that if a person wasn't qualified for the job or did something illegal, he certainly would take recommendations regarding qualified people to replace them. Otherwise, he wanted continuity at the county level in state government.

Not too long after the inauguration, I was approached by a gentleman named Odell Sipes from Hardeman County, a rural county in West Tennessee, where the largest employer was Western State Mental Hospital. Meeting in my office, Sipes said he had a list of the "hands" he wanted to fire and the hands he wanted to hire. With a straight face, I explained that it was a new day; we wouldn't do it that way anymore. I added that if anyone at the hospital wasn't performing satisfactorily, and if the hospital director agreed with him, we could look into replacing employees. Sipes was not enthusiastic.

I related that story to the Commissioner of Mental Health, Dr. Nat Winston, Jr., a charismatic psychiatrist from upper East Tennessee who later ran for governor on the Republican ticket. He invited me to Bolivar to visit the mental hospital and meet some of its employees. I could see the difficulties they had in attracting qualified doctors, not to mention lower-level staff such as nurses' aides and cleaning staff. It was an interesting exposure to that part of the state and a part of state government that I hadn't previously encountered. The state needed qualified hands. Period.

Did We Raise Taxes or Not?

In his first term, Gov. Ellington did not raise taxes at all. In his second campaign, he pledged not to raise the sales tax, which was the primary generator of taxes in our no income tax state. That has been an advantage—or disadvantage—depending on your political point of view.

After we got through the first legislative session, the governor said he wanted to make some things happen in education and elsewhere and asked us to find the financial wherewithal to make improvements. So, I got to work with the Commissioner of Finance Administration Harlan Mathews, and the Commissioner of Revenue, Tom Benson, and others. We put together what would end up being, at that time, the most significant tax increase in Tennessee's history. We raised every "sin tax" including beer and cigarette taxes. We raised the franchise and excise taxes. We raised the fees for different professional licenses, such as doctors and veterinarians. We didn't necessarily increase anything by substantial amounts, but we raised everything we could find that wasn't a sales tax.

The political reality was different then; there were lobbyists for these different groups that would bear the brunt of increasing revenue. So, we called each of them in: The business lobbyists who would get hit with the franchise and excise tax, the alcohol and cigarette people, plus the grocers who would also get hit with the sin tax, and the professional groups who would get hit with the license tax. The governor said, this is what we're going to do—I don't necessarily expect you to support it, but you're not going to fight it. He politically pressured the special interest groups to stay out of it, not in an illegal way but in a way that would be unheard of today.

The net revenue for the state was more than we would have generated by raising the sales tax by a penny.

Here's the reason why I phrased it as a question: Did we raise taxes or not? Gov. Ellington was known as a conservative Democrat who was judicious in spending state funds. Hudley Crockett, Ellington's press secretary and a television personality in Middle Tennessee, had decided to run in the Democratic Senate primary at the end of Ellington's term. His opponent was Albert Gore, Sr., who, as a liberal, was a bit out of touch with much of the state electorate. Crockett did some polling, and because he was publicly identified with the governor, one of the questions asked was whether Gov. Ellington had ever raised taxes.

More than 65% of the people polled responded that the Ellington administration never raised taxes. We had a reputation for being fiscally conservative, yet, we were able to implement one of the largest spending increases, particularly in higher education. It was an illuminating lesson in political perception versus reality. So, did we raise taxes or not? It depends on who you ask.

(Post note: Four years later, I first met Jake Butcher, when he was among the many strong Democratic candidates for governor in 1974. In the future, he would factor into my life in substantial and unforeseen ways. The then-mayor of Knoxville, Leonard Rogers, a friend of mine, set up a breakfast meeting with the three of us. Mayor Rogers just wanted me to get to know Jake, or J. B., as he was known then. As a vice president at UT, I explained that I wouldn't want to be involved directly in any political races. I was now part of a state institution, even though I had left the governor's office just a few years earlier. Butcher was very personable. I told him I would probably vote for Hudley Crockett in the primary, as he was my friend and colleague. Voters ended up electing Congressman Ray Blanton, who won with 35% of the vote, as Tennessee didn't have a runoff. Elements of the Blanton story will crop up here in different ways, as well.)

Switzerland Trip

In cooperation with their banking industry (perceived to be the epitome of no-questions-asked deposits), the government of Switzerland invited a selection of governors to be their guests for several days to share and compare methods of governance. Gov. Ellington and I were contacted by the National Governors' Conference (now Association), in which he was highly active and would eventually chair. We accepted the invitation, along with governors from New Jersey, Wisconsin, and Arizona.

Gov. Ellington didn't like to fly. I found that out one night when we'd flown together during the campaign. It was our first relatively lengthy flight on the state plane, a twin-engine aircraft. I had a long list of items to discuss once we reached cruising altitude, but all I heard from the governor was "harumph." He had his hand wrapped so tightly around a window curtain that his knuckles were white. We accomplished little on that flight.

I'm not sure if his fear of flying was an excuse or not, but the governor bowed out of the Switzerland trip and sent me as his representative. Our initial meetings began in Lucerne, and my flight there from Zurich was my first view of Europe. That small, bucolic city, nestled around Lake Lucerne, remains one of the most idyllic places I've ever seen, and I've now been all over the world. I remained in awe of the beauty of the country as we traveled to various meetings. We didn't have a strict formal schedule, but instead had discussions about their decentralized system of government in comparison to our combination of state and federal powers. Everywhere we went, wherever I turned my head or looked out a window, the view was picture-postcard perfect. And, it struck me that I could glimpse this unimaginable scenery because the Swiss did not permit the one thing which America has in abundance: Billboards. The views were unobstructed and picturesque. The Swiss values of preserving and cherishing their landscape is as striking as the landscape itself.

They also take great pride in their transportation system. As we traveled around by train, our hosts told us that while we were an important group of visitors, when the train was scheduled to leave, it was going to leave—whether we were on it or not. We visited the capital,

Bern, and the ski resort of Gstaad. While in Zurich, Switzerland's largest city, I asked one of our guides to direct me to the best place to purchase a Swiss watch. His reply? "Singapore," he said, explaining that one could buy a high-quality Swiss watch much cheaper there and without the duty taxes.

In Basel, we met with the mayor and the director of the Kunstmuseum Basel, which houses the oldest public art collection in the world. Its numerous Pablo Picasso artworks represent just one of the shining highlights of its deeply impressive holdings, but the story about its acquisition of six specific Picasso paintings and a drawing is legendary. So, how did the Kunstmuseum Basel come to own these particular works by the famed Spanish artist? In 1967, the Kunstmuseum was already exhibiting two of the Picasso paintings, which were on loan from the family foundation of wealthy collector Rudolf Staechelin. His son was the majority shareholder of Swiss charter operator Globe Air. Following a disastrous crash that killed 126 people, Globe Air was forced into bankruptcy. Staechelin found himself quickly deaccessioning significant artworks to access the substantial cash he needed to satisfy creditors. The family foundation had already sold two Picassos, along with works by Monet, Cézanne, Van Gogh, and Alfred Sisley.

Under extreme public pressure from young people and the museum's Director, Staechelin agreed to permit the city of Basel to acquire the two remaining Picassos for 8.4 million Swiss Francs (1.95 million U.S, dollars). The 1967 Basel painting referendum, which was championed by local youth and football club members, among others, would grant CHF6 million from the city with the requirement that the public raise the CHF2.4 million balance. The younger citizens, the art aficionados and the city visionaries banded together, and raised the money, bit by bit, through such quaint methods as shining shoes and selling popcorn. They exceeded the fundraising goal prior to the referendum vote, which passed 32,118 votes to 27,190 votes. The city also required the Staechelin Foundation to continue its long-term loan of other spectacular works from its collection for a minimum of 15 years. This was a city that valued art!

A fascinating addendum to this story is that Picasso was alive at the time, and had heard about Basel's fundraising effort. Charmed by the accompanying slogans like "All you need is Pablo"—the artist invited the museum Director to visit him in his studio overlooking Cannes in southeastern France. Picasso was said to have been so overwhelmed by the citizens' actions that he wanted to donate a painting. Pointing to two works of art on his wall, Picasso said, "I want you to pick either of these, and I will make that a gift to the youth of your city." The museum director was quite clever in deliberating between the two canvases, agonizing over the decision. He felt that the pair belonged together; Picasso's wife concurred. In the final analysis, Picasso donated both paintings, along with a painting from his Rose Period, and an important sketch of *Les Demoiselles d'Avignon*, which marked the turning point toward Cubism. In a concurrent act of generosity, a Swiss art collector and philanthropist then contributed another major Picasso, *The Poet*, 1912. The year 1967 was certainly the "Year of Picasso" for the city of Basel.

Afterward, I wondered if a similar referendum—using taxpayer money to purchase art from a private citizen—would ever pass in this country? I certainly don't believe it would happen in Tennessee. Probably not even in Manhattan. At any rate, I think a private buyer might have stepped up first in America.....whether to make the purchase for their personal collection or as a gift to the city to hang in its finest museum in perpetuity? Impossible to know.

Our group's final function was a formal luncheon in a castle on Lake Geneva. After a lavish seven-day tour, saying it was in a beautiful setting is redundant. Our party of eight was hosted by our traveling companions, along with officials from the Swiss banking association. As we started a more structured discussion with our after-dessert coffee, one of our hosts asked me as the sole representative of a Southern state, how we were dealing with our racial problems (it was 1967, and racial turmoil was boiling over). I began by stating that we certainly had problems and were addressing them with as much speed as possible, but that it was a difficult task. I told them that we were the first state in the south to have an African American in our cabinet, but that was only a start. I then said that the overriding division was deeper, but was not totally dissimilar to the class situation in Switzerland.

The silence that followed was deafening. I went on to say that I didn't mean to be disrespectful, but it would have been difficult in Switzerland for me to have represented a canton (their state equivalent) in another country. I came from a working-class background—my father was a truck driver who later operated three trucks—but I was able to earn a college degree and was then subsequently selected as chief of staff to a governor.

And, that reflected my evolving outlook, influenced so heavily by my first trip abroad and experiencing the postcard beauty of this

800-year-old country. I was almost overwhelmed by the beauty, the neatly trimmed roadways, the absence of billboards, the spotless and super-efficient railroads, and the seemingly universal high standard of living.

Yet, even with billboards spoiling many of our natural vistas, some weeds in the ditches along some roadways, and lack of nationwide passenger trains, let alone running on time, I continued to feel that my country was the best one in the world. No matter how enchanting I found Switzerland to be, I'd take America over any other.

MLK Assassination: Aftermath in the "Home State"

As the American Airlines jet gained altitude above National Airport (now Reagan) in Washington D.C., the view reminded me of photographs I had seen from WWII after a city had been bombed. Smoke from the fires of rioting in our nation's capital drifted skyward, etching an indelible image in my mind of April 5th, 1968.

I was heading back to my hotel room on the night of April 4th when I picked up several urgent messages asking me to call my office ASAP. That's when I learned the tragic news about Martin Luther King's assassination in Memphis at 6:05 p.m. (CST). The governor had decided to call out the National Guard in order to be ready to deal with the inevitable reactions that would be forthcoming. He received some criticism for reacting so quickly, which was characterized as heavy-handed in some quarters, but his instincts were correct.

Flights never departed National Airport after 10 p.m. in those days, so I was not able to return to Nashville until the following morning. Flying into Nashville on that Friday, I did not see the kind of smoke billowing as I had in Washington D.C. But, upon deplaning, I immediately sensed the tension crackling in the air. On the cab ride to the Executive Residence (where Command Central had been set up), I saw both National Guardsmen and some tanks parked along the roads in some areas. Traffic was light.

I was briefed by the Adjutant General and the Commissioner of Safety after arriving and continued to observe the evolving situation with Gov. Ellington as the day went on. No major confrontations developed in either Memphis or Nashville, the two Tennessee cities with the largest Black populations. As evening came, tensions began to increase. There were reports of trouble at Tennessee State University just a few miles from the Residence. The Adjutant General talked about some new "scopes" that his men had that enabled night vision. He went on to say, "I hope none of our boys get hurt."

I said, "I hope no one gets hurt." Then a palpable silence descended on the room filled with military and law enforcement-trained folks. Someone murmured, "Well, yeah, of course."

I realized later that I probably had made my one significant contribution.

We were criticized for the force of the response, but I will always be thankful that not a single life was lost and, unlike so many other cities and states, that there was very little damage, especially in the communities with great populations of Black citizens.

1968 and a Crazy, Raging Chicago

1968 was an unbelievably volatile year in American history. Almost every generation could name a pivotal year that challenged their very identity. I think 2020 was certainly another one of those years considering the Presidential election. Most of the turmoil of 1968 was related to the Vietnam War with the anti-war protests led by the hippies alongside racial strife. President Lyndon Johnson was criticized for escalating the war, then pilloried for not doing enough.

On March 31 that year, Johnson shocked the nation when he delivered his "Withdrawal Speech," informing Americans that he would not run for re-election. Miraculously, the speech wasn't leaked. The president said that with American troops risking their lives for the country every day in Vietnam, he couldn't spend even an hour worrying about a campaign, so there wouldn't be one for him. He said he planned to focus on dealing with the ongoing war. His announcement caused a seismic shift in the political landscape at a perilous time.

Back in November of 1967, Senator Eugene McCarthy had officially entered the Democratic primary to run against President Johnson. As we say in the South, that takes a lot of gumption and gall. It was unprecedented to take on an incumbent president from one's own party at that time, but McCarthy gathered a lot of support, particularly from young people disillusioned with the war and the state of the country.

It would be just a few months later that Martin Luther King would die in St. Joseph's Hospital in Memphis.

King's death further inflamed racial tensions, as Congress continued to expand the Civil Rights Act. The Vietnam War protests continued apace. President Kennedy's brother, the former U.S. attorney general, Robert Kennedy, entered the race for president and had just won the California Democratic primary in June. He was assassinated in Los Angeles on the way to deliver his victory speech. The killing of a second prominent political figure on the left side of the political aisle further stoked the anger, frustration, and dismay that was swelling throughout the country. Thus, it felt ironic to me that the "Establishment" candidate, supported by Johnson and his followers was Vice President Hubert Humphrey. Known as "the happy warrior," he was probably one of the more liberal members of the U.S. Senate when he represented Minnesota, prior to becoming vice president. Interestingly, he was generally viewed as the "conservative establishment" candidate by many.

As we approached the Democratic Convention in August in Chicago, McCarthy was still running strong when South Dakota Senator George McGovern entered the race. Rep. Hale Boggs of Louisiana, the House Majority Whip and an influential member of the Democratic Congressional Delegation, called Gov. Ellington, seeking assistance. Boggs headed the platform committee, which developed the Democratic platform for the convention (although the platform might be abandoned later; at the time, it was important). The governor asked me to attend, and I gladly accepted since the convention sounded like an exciting and interesting experience.

The televised committee meetings were in Washington D.C., just before the convention in August. It became quite a spectacle, particularly with the dynamic, headline-seeking congressman from San Francisco, Rep. Phil Burton in attendance. Burton was dominating and vicious in going after the administration and the cabinet members; he and others basically made everything about dealing with Vietnam, and racial unrest to a lesser extent, much more so than platform issues.

One of the most telling moments occurred when Secretary of State Dean Rusk was testifying before the committee. Appointed by President Johnson, he had been a widely respected, and a qualified diplomat who brought dignity and balance (I thought) to the State Department and as a representative of the administration. Rusk was getting so unmercifully grilled that it was almost difficult to watch, but he was a pro and handled himself with aplomb. During the intense interrogation, which was supposed to have been a Q&A, somebody came from backstage and tapped Rusk on the shoulder. As he listened, I could see his shoulders slump. Rusk turned back to the microphone, hesitated for a few seconds, and said he had to leave. The Soviet Union had just sent troops to invade Hungary, and he had to deal with that situation. That moment brought home to me that other things were occurring in the world, and that people carried other responsibilities wherever they went. It didn't offset any of the vitriolic reactions or attitudes in that room on that day, but it was sobering to me and, I think, to anybody in the room at that moment. At least temporarily.

We moved on to the convention in Chicago. Gov. Ellington headed the Tennessee delegation; I wasn't a delegate myself, but had staff credentials to attend the same events as the delegates. Those four days,

August 26th to 29th, saw one of the most riotous, literally, conventions that has ever taken place. Much of the ruckus occurred outside of the convention hall. Most of the delegates stayed in the Palmer Hotel. We walked back and forth to the convention center for meetings, but never felt unsafe. We were shielded by nearly wall-to-wall police protection outside. It was only later that we realized how tumultuous things actually were, once we had a chance to watch television and view the rioting in Grant Park and other places. The charges of police brutality seemed justified. The newscasts clearly showed the police attacking protesters and turning them into rioters; in many instances, they caused the riots. Chicago Mayor Richard J. Daley was perfectly cast as the bully. Though roundly mocked, he would do anything to control his city. It was a brutal undertaking with many bloodied heads and numerous people hospitalized. Amazingly, not a single death occurred outside of the convention hall, despite all of the rioting that took place.

Nothing in my previous political experience could have possibly prepared me for the convention itself.

As an "insider" on staff, I thought that most fictional portrayals of a convention on the television screen were, by and large, "B movies" stuff.

Tennessee had a prominent location in the hall because of its relationship with President Johnson. By the second session of the first day, the craziness erupted. The larger Massachusetts delegation was seated behind us, where noted economist, political activist and speaker John Kenneth Galbraith quickly established his presence. He sounded as if he was having a highly emotional fit, jeering, as he was hoisted back and forth over the standing Massachusetts delegation, which was clearly extremely distraught over the loss of another native Kennedy son. I saw people yelling from the floor and the balcony and thought, "I'm now living in a B-movie."

Watching democracy in action was a terribly painful experience (literally, in some cases, for the protestors). There was never a moment where everyone came together and united. Even the national anthem drew sitting protests. Ironically, the only quiet moments were outside, as we walked back to the hotel, flanked by police.

VP Humphrey was the nominee, and Senator Edmund Muskie of Maine, the vice presidential candidate.

As if the campaign of 1968 wasn't volatile enough, Alabama Governor George Wallace, a staunch segregationist, entered the race as a third-party candidate. Nixon won, of course, by less than 1% over Humphrey. Wallace earned nearly 10 million votes and 46 delegates. Those were *anti*-votes, not *anti-Vietnam* votes, necessarily; it was more likely they were racially motivated votes. I agree with most pundits who said the outcome would have been higher in favor of Nixon if Wallace hadn't run. In Tennessee, the outcome was Nixon with 47.6%, Wallace 34%, with Humphrey coming in third with 28.1%. Prior to that time, Tennessee had enjoyed a predominantly Democratic legislature for 50 years. It's hard to ascertain how much the national election affected things statewide, but the Republicans ended up with 49 members as did the Democrats. There was one independent from Knoxville who voted with the Republicans.

One of the reasons I bring that up is to show how bipartisanship continued in some places during those turbulent times. As a Democratic administration, we were going to be dealing with a Republican House of Representatives. The Speaker of the House was a Republican friend of ours, Bill Jenkins, from the small city of Rogersville in upper East Tennessee. As the state government, we really didn't miss a beat. The leadership from the Republican House and the Democratic Senate would get together in the governor's office and review the agenda. When a partisan issue would arise, each side would negotiate their respective positions, and then we'd get back together to address the state's problems and opportunities. This bipartisanship was so reflective of the times: we had many strong Republican friends in both houses, who were important contributors to policies and laws, and who supported our tax programs earlier in 1968 when the Democrats were in control. Some of the republicans who put the best interests of the state first, in addition to Speaker Jenkins, were Senators Tommy Garland, Ben Atchley, Tommy Haun from East Tennessee and Leonard Dunavant from Memphis, along with Representatives Tom Jensen and David Copeland. While 1968 was one of the most volatile years in American politics, we found common ground in Tennessee.

Some of the Good News in 1968

Every Monday morning, Gov. Ellington, had breakfast with his long-time doctor and friend, Thomas Frist, Sr.

Ellington even asked me to join them occasionally at the Hermitage Hotel, which was always an enlightening experience. One of the topics that came up frequently was Dr. Frist's plan to propose a new kind of private health care system. Because I clearly saw Dr. Frist's genuine dedication to his profession, I took advantage of our acquaintance and his good nature by asking if we might bring my mother-in-law to Park West (his hospital) for some tests. Her health was rapidly declining. The latest technological advancements revealed that her liver was barely functioning, a condition that would result in death, if untreated. Her doctors in the small town of Harriman, where she lived, had not accurately diagnosed her disease. Some quick treatments and an overhaul of unhealthy habits, quickly put her on the road to recovery. At that point, my affiliation with the Frists had become very personal. Our family could not have been more grateful.

I didn't fully understand the soon-to-be-felt impact of Dr. Frist's private venture, the Hospital Corporation of America (HCA). In 1968 the first stock was offered, and I was fortunate to be able to buy 200 shares. Within a short time, it doubled in value. Like a small-time investor, I sold it because the gains were a big deal to me. Every time I give in to stewing about "what might have been" if I'd held on to that stock, I was reminded of the sage advice I received from another of Gov. Ellington's friends, banker Sam Hunt, who said: "When you sell at a profit, don't ever look back."

The HCA "idea" I heard discussed over breakfast resulted in thousands of jobs, in millions of patients treated worldwide, and in Nashville becoming a multi-billion-dollar, international health-care center. It also provided the Frist family with the wherewithal to become a group of gracious, generous philanthropists, funding causes in Nashville, in Tennessee and farther afield. Despite the tenor of the times, there were some extraordinarily good things happening in 1968.

The Feds Are Coming! The Feds Are Coming!

President Johnson and Gov. Ellington were very close friends. Following President Kennedy's assassination, Johnson worked on passing the progressive programs that Kennedy had initiated in Congress. He had the ability to push the massive "The Great Society" legislation through congress. So, large amounts of federal funds were becoming available for new programs in housing, law enforcement, and urban development. Tennessee was at the front of the line, so to speak. We were going to get our fair share and, whenever possible, even more. However, many of the programs were designed to be multidisciplinary or didn't fit neatly into a particular department, such as the department of highways or safety. I set up the Office of Urban and Federal Affairs, a new administration office to handle many of these new programs. For the director, I hired Dr. Hyrum Plaas, a man I didn't know well, but one who came highly recommended by UT's political science department. He was a good man, very bright; but, as an educator, he was far better versed in theory than in practice, and, consequently, had little patience for the give-and-take of the political process. His tenure was short-lived.

We quickly promoted his assistant, Walter Lambert, to director of the new office. Lambert, who had headed the highway safety program, was a down-to-earth, good ol' boy from East Tennessee. He was a doctoral student at UT, who, we jokingly said, we kept so busy that he stopped pursuing his doctorate after receiving his master's in political science, because we left him no time to complete his Ph.d work.

We became very close associates and personal friends. He worked for me several times in different capacities at UT, and then later at the

World's Fair, as well. Additionally, we hired a bunch of other young whippersnappers, professionals in various fields, who excelled at directing grants to the right people or the right programs. Lambert's assistant director was a young man from Middle Tennessee, Leonard Bradley, another sharp guy who worked in several of the new areas and eventually succeeded Lambert as director.

Toward the end of the administration, with Gov. Ellington's support, I set up a transition program, something that certainly didn't exist when Gov. Clement came in (of course, less of a transition was needed due to the "leapfrog" of the Ellington and Clement administrations). This was going to be a more substantial transition regardless of who was elected. It was especially important when Winfield Dunn was elected—the state's first Republican governor in 50 years. His victory was the result of a substantial number of crossover votes, cast by Democrats who simply couldn't support the liberal positions of Democrat John Jay Hooker.

I assigned Bradley to oversee the transition effort. The last six months when I was in the governor's office—the final part of Ellington's term—I knew I was going back to UT, where I would eventually be offered the position of vice president. But, the university wanted me to start right away, while the governor wanted me to stay. So, I divided my time, and essentially had two part-time jobs, which were really two full-time jobs. During the transition, I was flying back and forth with the incoming Republicans, giving them briefings and becoming close friends with many of them. I wanted to showcase Bradley and his young colleagues, so we included them in different meetings. The Dunn administration quickly recognized their collective brilliance and retained them all, mostly in the same office. They were highly energetic, competent professionals, knew the territory and were eager to continue serving their state.

The Female Power That Kept Government Running

The first "computer" I ever knew was Mary Smith, who was Gov. Ellington's executive secretary. This quiet, distinguished-looking lady had served Gov. Clement throughout his three terms, and Gov. Ellington in his first term. It didn't take me too long to realize how much her knowledge, her judgment, her unswerving, yet openly honest loyalty, along with a work ethic that put the rest of us to shame, meant to the efficiency and competency of the state's chief executive officer. I was awed watching her sort through the volume of mail we received every day, knowing precisely when to draft the response herself, when to route it to an appropriate staff person, and when to follow-up to be certain that it was acted upon, all while never, ever coming close to showing even a scintilla of frustration or irritation. Gov. Winfield Dunn, who succeeded Gov. Ellington, remarked in his memoir that the biggest mistake he made was in not taking Ellington's advice and keeping Mary Smith in his office.

My teenage assistant during the campaign, Claudia Seabolt (now Viking), was fortunate to work with Ms. Smith prior to rejoining me in my office later in the term. She then served as a part-time aide to me at UT, while finishing her degree and going on to a venerable career in journalism. Like me, Seabolt was an ardent admirer of Mary Smith.

Another learning experience for me was working with, and also ob-serving the legion of uber-competent women who kept the enormous wheels of state government operating. We had two female commis-sioners, Gwendolyn Davis from Lebanon, who served as Commission-er of Personnel, and Josie Burson of Memphis, the Commissioner of Employment Security. Both ladies executed their duties with exem-plary grace and distinction. Unlike some other departments, we never had a problem during their entire four years of service. Mrs. Bur-son's son, Charles, an active student volunteer during our campaign, became Tennessee's Attorney General, before moving to Washington to serve as Chief of Staff to then-Vice President Albert Gore.

Other outstanding examples of the ladies who "made the history happen" in the governor's office included: Virginia Sawdey, Yvonne Woods, and my first assistant, Kenny Long. A cadre of "treasures" who kept the constitutional side of things moving were Betty Brown, Bebe Zucarello, and Virginia Andes. And, then there was Margaret Tolleson, who knew almost as much or more about the office of Ten-nessee's Secretary of State as anyone anywhere. She had been em-ployed there for some five decades. When that office was relocated to the space that I had occupied in the State Capitol, I would always go by and check to make sure that it was being taken care of with appropri-ate reverence. I was proud to count Ms. Margaret, and the other ladies, as exemplary human beings and cherished friends.

As I transitioned to UT, I was lucky to associate with another cadre of competent women. The "Mary Smith" of UT was Betty Davis, who served as assistant to both Presidents Holt and Boling, while among those keeping me and others ``running straight" were Libby Pritchett, Katie Barber, and Betty Tinker.

There were many other unsung heroes at UTK, as there were in Nashville; my list just includes the ones with whom I was fortunate enough to interact on a regular basis. As a society, we are still battling to ensure equality and appropriate recognition for the contributions of women. It's truly a noble cause.

One Piece of Advice, If Asked

It's a great privilege to serve in an elected or appointed position at any level of government. Though occasionally discussed, I never ran for office, but, I wholeheartedly admire any citizen who takes the step to offer themselves for public service. Quite often, friends would ask to meet with me when they were considering undertaking a political race. The first question I always pose is this one: "Are you prepared to lose?" Unless they had made this leap at any time prior to our conversation, I would generally receive a quizzical look that conveyed the question they were thinking: "Why would you ask that?" I told every would-be candidate the same thing. Running for office is a very personal experience. I have consoled countless mothers, fathers, sons and daughters, all of them heartbroken following a friend or family member's loss in a race for public office. It's exhilarating, exhausting, personal, and completely gut-wrenching; like a sports contest, it can either evoke the soaring thrill of victory or the searing agony of defeat. Regardless, the experience will be forever emblazoned on the psyche of all involved.

I was fortunate enough to be part of Gov. Ellington's especially hard-fought primary victory in his final gubernatorial race and lucky to join his cabinet of advisors. As a young, ambitious turk. I had the particular privilege of serving with a man of immense wisdom, deep experience and ample compassion. While he was a serious taskmaster who required much from his staff, he generously supported us and promoted us whenever appropriate and possible. Loyalty was mandatory. However, he qualified that by regularly reminding us "that if we are agreeing all of the time, then one of us isn't thinking."

The governor and I had an extremely close relationship. We both knew that if either of us made a mistake, we still had each other's back, no questions asked.

Regarding the advice that I used to caption this section, I offered it when solicited, and occasionally, gave it without being asked, such as when one who had a responsibility to a governor or a mayor: Take time to savor the moment. During the four or eight years in office, take a few minutes every week, or every month, or at least on some regular basis, to take a breath, walk out to a real (or figurative) balcony, and drink in the fresh air of freedom, responsibility and exceptional opportunity that has been presented. Say grace and give thanks for the privilege that accompanies the potential for making a real difference. Trust me, time races faster than Pheidippides. Savor it.

The Ellington years.
*Photo courtesy of the
Tennessee State Library
and Archives.*

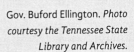

Gov. Buford Ellington. *Photo
courtesy the Tennessee State
Library and Archives.*

Gov. Ellington, at the podium, introduces President Lyndon B. Johnson during the president's visit to Nashville. *Photo courtesy the Tennessee State Library and Archives.*

6

....

THE UT YEARS: YOUNGEST VICE PRESIDENT JOINS ANDY, ED, AND JOE

....

Young Turk Taken In, and Back Again

During those last six months, when I straddled the Ellington administration and UT, my official title was executive assistant to the aforementioned Dr. Andy Holt, who was the president of UT at that time but had already announced his retirement. One of the most delightful people I've ever known, Dr. Holt presided over UT at about the same time as Gov. Clement first took office in the late 1950s. He was one of the few non-agricultural presidents of that land grant institution, and he brought in aggressive people. Dr. Ed Boling, who was Gov. Clement's first budget director, and later Commissioner of Finance when they reorganized state government, was Holt's vice president. Boling, who would soon succeed Holt as president, would be my boss when I was promoted to vice president (It was an enterprising student reporter at UT's student-operated *Daily Beacon* who researched and revealed that I was the youngest person to be named a Vice President at UT. Thus, the *youngest* streak continued.)

It was not a difficult transition from working with UT in a gubernatorial capacity with the governor's office to working with them as colleagues, albeit with different duties. I was welcomed back, and it felt good to be there.

Dr. Joe Johnson, who had been Gov. Ellington's assistant and then Assistant Commissioner of Finance, was one of the professionals Dr. Holt hired. Also a vice president, Dr. Johnson handled development and external matters and relationships with the legislature and administration, often going to Nashville during the legislative session. Unfortunately, right after I started there, we had some problems with our Medical Institute in Memphis, a campus that contained medical, dental, pharmaceutical, and nursing schools. Johnson was dispatched there as interim chancellor to straighten out the administrative problems. I was sent back to Nashville to lobby for UT. I hadn't planned on returning to the State Capitol, but I was back there again, sans office, talking to people.

We had some difficulties with the Speaker of the House at that time, especially with the Democrats bucking tradition by ignoring the Republican governor-elect's choices for constitutional officers. The Democratic Caucus nominated a gentleman from Nashville, Jim McKinney, as Speaker of the House. My beloved Volunteers had a good team that year and were facing the Air Force in the Sugar Bowl in New Orleans. I was in charge of organizing the VIPs and invitees for the official party, including the governor, governor-elect, and speaker-elect. As we picked everyone up at the airport, McKinney raised holy hell over a minor detail. He noticed that Governor-elect Dunn's limo was slightly longer than his, demonstrating what a "big man" he was, politically. His obsession with those kinds of details did not serve him well.

McKinney wasn't enthusiastic about the UT system, and seemed to harbor a general distrust of both me and UT. I thought he might have been influenced by his status as a Tennessee Tech grad, and as a fan of TTU President Derryberry, but that was sheer speculation on my part. However, he had a cousin who wanted to attend the UT medical school. I sent the request to interim-chancellor Johnson, who tried to accommodate him, but McKinney's cousin simply didn't qualify for medical school. McKinney was not happy. So, I had to deal with a legislature where the House Speaker didn't care for either UT or me. Anytime a bill related to UT came up in a committee, McKinney would appear. For those who haven't worked with legislators, though the speaker may be a member of all committees, it's fairly ominous for that person to join a committee meeting. McKinney would enter and say, "I hear this is something about UT, so I'm here to defeat it." That was the antagonistic atmosphere in which I worked for a few years.

Despite that, one of the things that Tennessee has prided itself on, going back to my UT days and the Clement–Ellington terms, was in hiring professionals and nonpartisan people to operate the offices.The year that Governor Dunn was elected, the Democrats had taken back control of the House and continued controlling the Senate.

The way Tennessee's system works is that the party caucuses get together prior to the inauguration. The governor has a major input as to who will be selected as the constitutional officers—such as secretary of state, comptroller, and treasurer. The legislature then makes its choice from those nominees. Well, there was going to be no input from the governor this time—because he was a Republican.

In 1973, a younger, more activist group of liberals took control of the House Democratic Caucus. Rather than re-nominating Bill Snodgrass as comptroller, they nominated a younger Democrat, Floyd Kephart, a smart, but partisan guy with no accounting background. That would have been a major shift in direction in terms of state government *if* it had occurred. The only reason it didn't happen is because a friend of mine who was in the governor's office joined with the moderate Democrats and 100% of the Republicans. Because those constitutional officers are elected by a majority of Senate and House voting together, not as separate bodies, they had enough votes to reject the Democratic caucus nominee and re-elected Snodgrass. He remained comptroller until 1999. When he retired, the largest state office building in Nashville was named the William R. Snodgrass Tower. The maneuverings to keep him in office were an increasingly rare example of Democrats and Republicans taking the "nuclear option" together. Sometimes that's what it takes to maintain vigorous fiscal management in a state.

Just as Bill Snodgrass was a prime example of professionals migrating from UT to state government, another example was Roy S. Nicks. Like Joe Johnson, Nicks was a product of the Southern Regional Training Program, a unique, masters-level public administration degree with studies at UT, and the universities of Alabama and Kentucky. Dr. Nicks served as Commissioner of Public Welfare under Gov. Clement, was Chancellor of the UT Nashville campus, before becoming Chancellor of the Board of Regents. He capped his career in higher education when he was recruited as president of East Tennessee State University. Even with all of his accomplishments, he said his major contribution to the state was when he and Joe Johnson talked Commissioner of Finance and Administration (F & A) Harlan Mathews into hiring a young, fellow Southern Regional Training Program graduate named Jerry Adams. He went on to serve as second-in-command at F & A under 10 governors, and was heralded throughout the nation for his budgetary expertise, while providing the continuity under which Tennessee's fiscal policies thrived.

Creating the Institute for Public Service in a Smoke-filled Room

While winding down my four years with Gov. Buford Ellington and transitioning back to UT, I spent the last six months of his administration "half-time" with the governor and "half-time" with UT. Initially this sounded like a reasonable plan except, as it turned out, I wound up doing two full-time jobs.

The holidays also illustrated the political realities of a typical departure from government power. The first three Christmases at the Capitol, I could barely get in my office, filled as it was with all the hams, candy, and spirits. (The telephone company, a more reserved entity, always sent a monogrammed leather folder or a Dopp kit.) At that time, these gifts were legal, albeit with limits on what lobbyists could send.

On the final holiday of the Ellington administration, which was 18 or so days before the inauguration of the incoming governor, I received just two Christmas cards: One with my name misspelled and the other stamped, "postage due." While the lobbyists liked what I represented, I didn't represent *that* anymore. Smart lobbyists that they were, they transferred their laser-focused attention to the future. Among the most fundamental of lessons that I learned from Governor Ellington was to recognize and prepare for the inevitability of the shifting winds that are always on the horizon.

In any event, it was an enjoyable, if occasionally, hectic time. One of the ideas that had been discussed with UT President Andy Holt (who was retiring) and soon-to-be incoming president Ed Boling was to create a new, umbrella organization consisting of the multitude of public service operations which were integral parts of UT's mission. I wanted to consolidate and combine them into one organization, similar to the Institute of Agriculture, which, along with education and public service, was part of the three-pronged objective of our state's land-grant university. I thought it could be appropriately named the Institute for Public Service.

Prior to finishing with the governor in mid-January and starting full-time at UT, I decided to take some time during the holiday break to give myself space to think about and draft a paper to present to the UT Board of Trustees in January. The perfect place for the solitude that I would need to do this was my in-laws' lakeside cabin in Roane County. Taking the requisite groceries and supplies with me, I planned to spend three days developing the paper.

On my first, frigid night there, while making dinner, I decided to light the picturesque fireplace. The good news was that it blazed instantly; the bad news was that I had neglected to fully open the flue. Almost instantly, the room was filled with smoke. I banged and pulled, trying everything I could think of, all to no avail.

Finally, I threw open all of the windows and doors and made it out to the front porch. Sitting there, shivering, wearing every coat I had brought and could find, I realized that I'd neglected the cardinal rule of fire making: be certain that you can operate the flue before striking a match. This incident occurred long before cell phones were invented, so I couldn't contact my in-laws for assistance. I just had to wait it out.

Later, while sipping a much-needed glass of wine, I got to thinking: A university is, hopefully, made up of educated people who have a lot to offer students and citizens throughout the state. I was soon to become a full-time vice president there. I was working on a paper that would initiate a major change for the university and, ultimately, benefit the state, but I lacked the ability to accomplish something so rudimentary? Hmmm. At that moment, I was quite happy to be alone. I would decide later whether or not to share this laughable incident with friends, let alone the skeptics who already had qualms about this young guy from Harriman with the newfangled ideas.

The aim of public service at a university is to take the knowledge, experience, and innovation of faculties and students in various disciplines and apply that expertise to benefit its state's private and public sectors. Despite apparent shortcomings in some practical applications of life, I thought my idea of creating a "big umbrella" was a worthy one.

The existing agencies included the Municipal Technical Advisory Service, formed to directly assist city and municipal governments.

Staff, interns, and faculty research addressed the short and long-term needs of cities. Similarly, there was the Center for County Government Services, which assisted the 95 county governments in Tennessee, and the Center for Industrial Services, available for research and assistance in the private sector.

More recently, a Center for Government Training had been set up to provide structured, professional training courses for state government departments. It was a priority of Comptroller Snodgrass, who had dedicated his career to better government. When I completed the paper, President Holt and Dr. Boling and his staff signed off. The Board of Trustees unanimously adopted the report and established the UT Institute of Public Service later that year.

When the board met and gave its approval, I laughed privately, thinking it might not have been a phoenix rising from the ashes, but it sure had some similarities.

Changing Times: Unrest, UT Nashville No More, Second Medical School Looms

Despite how beneficial the University of Tennessee has been over the years, some adversity has arisen from time to time. By an act of the state legislature, UT was directed to develop a campus in Nashville focused on training programs for state and local government employees. A new building was constructed less than a mile from the Capitol building, an elegant structure when it opened. Training courses were established, as well as academic programs specific to a master's degree program in public administration. Courses were to be offered in the evening, so that working government employees could easily attend.

Soon after its debut, a lawsuit was filed on behalf of Tennessee State University (then Tennessee A & I University) indicating the school's position that UT's presence in Nashville violated its rights. The lead attorney in the lawsuit was George Barrett; he and his firm had long been devoted to civil rights activities. Years later, Barrett and I became friends, and I became a great admirer, though when he was accusing UT as being a villain, we were not necessarily on friendly terms.

The lawsuit dragged on for at least two years. Eventually, there was an historic court ruling stating that UT had, in fact, violated the rights of TSU; that UT should cease operations, and that the property should be transferred to TSU. Now called the Avon Williams campus of TSU, both undergraduate and graduate classes are offered in the daytime and evenings. TSU's College of Business is headquartered there.

Another major effort of the state legislature, particularly from the upper East Tennessee legislative delegation, was the move to establish an additional medical school in Tennessee. This initiative went on for at least three sessions of the legislature; the first two were when I was in charge of working with the general assembly while Dr. Johnson was on assignment as Chancellor of the UT Medical Units in Memphis. The UT administration was not in favor of the proposal (and, there-fore, I was not in favor of it) primarily because the medical units op-erated by the UT in Memphis were grossly underfunded, despite pro-ducing more doctors than almost any medical school in the country. Gov. Winfield Dunn, a Memphis dental college graduate, heard our reasoning and was generally supportive.

Though we were able to delay any major progress that first year in the legislature, it became obvious that the medical school would be the focus of upper East Tennessee legislators. They were strongly united, would vote as a block, and would negotiate and trade votes with other legislators, so that eventually they were going to have enough votes to pass it. During the second legislative session, they successfully passed it, but after Dr. Ed Boling and I met with Gov. Dunn at the Executive Residence, we convinced him to veto the effort. Even though the governor's veto could be overridden by a mere majority of 51 votes in the house and 17 votes in the Senate, no effort was made that year to override the veto. (This veto, however, came back to haunt Gov. Dunn when he ran again for governor against House Speaker Ned Ray McWherter in 1992. The first congressional district, which is heavily Republican, voted overwhelmingly for Democrat McWherter, who served two consecutive terms as the state's Chief Executive and was named the most outstanding governor in the U.S. by *Governing* magazine in 1994.)

During the next legislative session, when Dr. Johnson was back in Knoxville and working with the legislature, the General Assembly again passed the bill to establish the medical school, but also included a major increase in funding for UT Medical Units in Memphis. At that point, UT could support the effort because the additional funding would put UT in a competitive position in the Southeast and nationally. We had never been against a new medical school, but we argued, "How could the state establish a new med school while grossly underfunding the school that already existed?" A coalition of legislators from upper East Tennessee, the Memphis area, and other UT supporters came together to work out an equitable solution allowing everyone to move forward.

Over the years, I would kid Joe Johnson that my efforts kept the second medical school from happening, but that during his first year back working with the General Assembly, we had an additional medical school.

An interesting side note to follow-up to the establishment of the new medical school involved U.S. Congressman Jimmy Quillen, who represented the first congressional district in upper East Tennessee for 34 years. He was a formidable force throughout the entire state legislative effort. As the unrelenting driver in the establishment of the new medical school, it was later named the East Tennessee State University James H. Quillen College of Medicine.

The episode occurred in fall 1973 when UT was to premiere its first home football game under lights. The opening game was against the defending national champions, Penn State University. Though it was to be televised, it was the largest ticket demand ever experienced by UT. As with the Sugar Bowl, I oversaw the VIP tickets for legislators, congressmen, senators, select others, and their guests. We had a limited number of available tickets, but could typically accommodate all requests. Most of the tickets were in the lower level 50-yard line section at Neyland Stadium. As noted, the demand for this game was beyond over-the-top.

Quillen's office called regularly to request tickets to home games. As far as anyone remembered, though, Congressman Quillen never personally attended a game but used the tickets for constituents in his district. Because I incorrectly assumed that these tickets would be the standard use for the Congressman, I placed his four tickets in the upper deck area near the end zone. They weren't awful seats, but they weren't the 50-yard line seats received by the majority of the VIPs.

The following Monday morning, I received a call from Congressman Quillen himself, who was livid. He had attended the game and brought some important guests with him. He was embarrassed and furious about being placed in less-than excellent seats. He blamed me and the university because of our opposition to the proposed medical school, and thought we had put him there to spite him. I assured him that was not the case and explained the situation— to no avail. We didn't have much interaction after that, and I don't think I ever convinced him that his conclusion was incorrect. To my knowledge, that was the only game he ever attended during his years in Congress. Talk about mixing politics and sports (and education?) to the ultimate degree ... .shows what happens when one inadvertently overlooks asking the most crucial question. In this case, it was, "Will you be joining us personally, Congressman?"

Creating a School: How Deans Lacy and Church Fostered a New School of Architecture and Touched so Many Lives

The architecture school at UT was coming to fruition during my first "tour of duty" at the university in 1965. The administration hired an outstanding dean in Bill N. Lacy, who had been the assistant dean at Rice University in Houston. Dean Lacy strongly believed in professors who were also practicing architects. He did the same himself throughout his storied 50-year career, designing many notable buildings, and advising prominent clients such as the J. Paul Getty Trust, where he chaired the Architect Selection Committee for the Getty Museum complex. Lacy was also a magnet for attracting superior candidates, mostly Tennesseans, along with others from around the country. He got the school off to a fast start. We had fun together, and I supported his vision and his very original ideas. One of the students at the time, Charlie Smith, was fondly nicknamed "Mr. Architect;" his is a name that will come up again and again, as I recount highlights from the World's Fair.

Another local architect, Bob Church, who became a close friend when I was in the governor's office, had received the contracts to design several state buildings. I remember the state architect telling me that when Church was preparing to design the community college in my home county (Roane), he spent time sitting quietly in the hills, imagining where structures should be sited on such a natural canvas. Church, too, was a practicing architect; in fact, he would become the next dean of UT's architecture school.

The two of us found an abundance of common ground regarding the gridiron. A football player at Georgia Tech, his enthusiasm for the game was equal to mine, which went far beyond normal fandom. Once, during a trip to New York when UT was participating in a basketball tournament at Madison Square Garden, he provided me with the architectural tour of a lifetime. To see the buildings of one of the incomparable cities of the world through the eyes of such a talented architect, was priceless. I would categorize it as one of my most eventful experiences in a life filled with truly memorable moments. Unfortunately, Church died way too young. He was in his forties when he suffered a heart attack on the handball court.

Despite the loss of Church, it was inspiring to watch the architecture school come to life and to feel the creative spirit with which they so infused it. To this day, one still senses the liveliness and creativity of that timeless space. It's an appropriate tribute to the pair of gentlemen who built it—Bill Lacy and Bob Church.

Simply the Best: Andy, Ed, and Joe

In the days before Andy Holt, UT was primarily a traditional, agriculturally oriented school (not a bad thing, but that's an accurate assessment). The school's fundraising was also a bit rooted in the past, with money only coming in through the alumni association. Members contributed $5 annually, and saw one another at get-togethers from time-to-time.

Dr. Holt understood that the meager tuition at that point didn't raise a lot of money, but that private funds were the key to making a real difference; what he called "the icing on the cake." When he brought in Ed Boling, he wanted him to serve as vice president of development, which included fundraising, a position that had never existed prior to this time. Boling began by assessing which public universities in the U.S. were the most adept at raising private dollars. There weren't many, but the University of Michigan (UM) was far and away the superior example. Boling then spent nearly six months studying that institution's fundraising operations and adapted their system to UT. At its core, UM was grounded in developing contacts, creating friendships, and pursuing solid, lasting relationships, both corporate and individual. These are standard methods now employed by most universities, but it was new ground at UT at that time.

One of the greatest fundraising successes came from Clarence Brown, a 1917 engineering school graduate who'd gone west and become a pioneer in the burgeoning film industry. The last movie he directed, *The Yearling*, was nominated for several Academy Awards and won three Oscars. He had also bought an extensive number of properties in Los Angeles and amassed tremendous wealth. Dr. Holt cultivated a relationship with Brown, who became the primary donor for the Clarence Brown Theatre on the Knoxville campus. This illustrates the results that Holt, Boling, and, later, Johnson, achieved with their revitalized fundraising efforts.

When Boling became president, Johnson was going to take over as vice president of development, but he had to attend to the aforementioned situation in Memphis. I took over fundraising for a few years and gleaned a few facts about bringing in the big bucks. I learned that the key to a public institution raising private money is for its President to be heavily invested and committed to personally making the "ask" when the time is right. Exceptional staff, solid research, and terrific programs all contribute to success when the head person devotes their time closing the deals. I was honored to work with such savvy professionals as Charlie Brakebill, and young staffers on their way to impressive careers, such as Phil Converse, Lofton Stuart, and Tom Ballard.

Eventually, UT earned a reputation, at least throughout the Southeast, for regularly surpassing other public institutions in securing private donations. That was attributable to the extraordinary work ethic of Holt, Boling and Johnson—all three doctorate holders, all three eventual UT presidents—bringing professionalism and progress to state institutions.

Interregnum

I was friends with former South Carolina Governor Bob McNair who was a lawyer and businessman. He was involved in a project involving the UT Hospital, which was across the river from the main campus, but not easily accessible. The university had worked with the state to build an intersection off Alcoa Highway (the major transportation artery to the airport), in order to improve access to the hospital. That construction project also provided better access to an adjacent property, which came to be known as Cherokee Bluff. McNair and a partner, the largest contractor in South Carolina, bought the property, and, as a personal favor, I connected them with area business people who could facilitate its development. They then asked if I wanted to run the Cherokee Bluff project.

After four years at UT, while still enjoying my work there, things were beginning to feel slightly repetitive. I decided to depart, left on good terms and accepted McNair's offer. Cherokee Bluff, with an outstanding view overlooking Knoxville and the Tennessee River, was the city's first condominium project. We hired McCarty Bullock Holsaple as the architects of record, which included Charlie Smith (I would soon work with them again). Over the course of a year-and-a-half, we developed a successful project, despite some financial difficulties. We had no problem securing construction funding, but due to the economic challenges nationally, the arrangements with the mortgage lender for purchaser financing were voided. We ended up relinquishing the project to our financier with access to mortgage financing in order to achieve its completion.

In the meantime, I had been talking to Ed Boling about a potential return to UT. I'd also become active in the community as a new "businessman." The mayor, Kyle Testerman, appointed me to the planning commission; and, I got involved in the United Way fundraising drive and became the chair of the budget committee.

Testerman was an aggressive, successful businessman who brought his energy to public service when he was elected Knoxville's 62nd mayor in 1972. A lifelong Republican, he was hard-nosed but progressive. As Testerman was preparing for the upcoming mayoral election (a nonpartisan race in Knoxville), another friend, Randy Tyree, a former policeman known for his campus drug busts had also decided to run for mayor.

Tyree had worked for me indirectly as assistant head of the Governor's Highway Safety Office, so I had gotten to know both him and his wife, Mary Pat. I spent an entire afternoon in a local restaurant trying to talk him out of running. I told Tyree he only had five strikes against him going in: the incumbent mayor, the Republican Party, the Democratic Party, and both Knoxville newspapers—other than that, I jokingly described his chances as good. Tyree said he sensed dissatisfaction among the electorate, as he felt that the working man was being overlooked by the mayor's office. As a small consolation, I said that if he decided to pursue his folly that I would quietly vote for him, but that I couldn't be associated with his campaign, since Testerman had been good to me.

Tyree needed funding for the campaign, so I joined with some other friends to sign a note for $30,000, which was not an insubstantial amount of money at the time. As the financiers, we kept our identity secret, but word soon got out. Testerman's campaign began asking, "Who are these unholy seven?" I was eventually revealed to be among them. Predictably, my relationship with Testerman was shaken, but somehow survived.

The first vote for mayor was shockingly close. The winner had to get 50% plus one vote. Testerman fell 37 votes short. In the subsequent runoff, Tyree pulled off an astounding upset victory. I then helped him reorganize the mayor's office.

7

THE BEGINNING OF THE QUEST

Near the end of Testerman's term, there had been talk of bringing an international exposition to Knoxville. He created a World's Fair committee to pursue a Special Category (themed) International Exposition to be held in 1980 (many have forgotten that was the event's original target year), but it was abandoned for myriad reasons.

The first I heard regarding a World's Fair was from Stewart Evans. He was head of the Downtown Knoxville Association, an organization of private businesses that had been shrinking in numbers as the city's population and business opportunities spread out to the suburbs, which, in Knoxville, simply meant going westward. Evans was lively, energetic, and a man of many ideas over the years. He was one of the hardest-working, most idealistic fellows I'd ever encountered. He was always conceiving new projects and ways to attract people (back?) downtown.

Even though he had a reputation for proposing ideas that rarely saw the light of day, Evans was rarely daunted and, seemingly, never discouraged. I don't know the details of his first meeting with then-mayor

Testerman, but Evans got his attention, and the ball started rolling. As events unfolded, Evans' role did not evolve into that of "lead" actor, but, as far as I know, he never complained. I generally try to refrain from making too many unequivocal statements, but here's one that I can make, without hesitation: THERE WOULD NOT HAVE BEEN A WORLD'S FAIR IN KNOXVILLE WITHOUT THE TENACITY AND FORWARD THINKING OF STEWART EVANS.

Unbeknownst to most of us, Evans attended the International Exposition in Spokane, Washington, in 1974. The president of Expo '74, a man named King Cole (yes, that was his actual name), had been Spokane's Downtown Association director, like Evans was in Knoxville. One of the first accomplishments in this endeavor was Evans' ability to coax Cole into coming to Knoxville to meet with the early Fair proponents. The collective wisdom of Mayor Testerman, Jake Butcher, and Jim Haslam led to Cole signing a long-term consulting agreement, which saved the project an inordinate amount of time and considerable money.

Spokane, at that time, had the distinction of being the smallest city to ever undertake such a major international event. As Knoxville was and is still larger, Spokane may be clinging to that title even today. Spokane's theme was the environment, and its site was along the waterfront. The goal there was to "give the Columbia River back" to the people of eastern Washington state. It was a resounding success. Evans returned home to Knoxville bubbling with excitement and passion. At first blush, one might think, "Alright, another one of Stewart's wild ideas." But the more I thought about it and looked at it, the more I, like other citizens, thought, well, why not take a look?

The Department of Commerce, with its multiple layers of government bureaucracy, was the approving body for a World's Fair. We had the mayor's office, the Chamber of Commerce, UT, the Tennessee Valley Authority, Union Carbide (the operator of the Oak Ridge National Laboratory through a federal contract), and many others all involved in seeking official approval.

The World's Fair committee determined that it wanted two things: one central point of contact to serve as the hub of a many-spoked wheel and that the most efficient way to operate the Fair would be to create a non-profit corporation. That's when I was asked to serve as the point person. It made sense; I was fairly young, was well-known in the community and had good working relationships with both political parties and business figures throughout the state. Now, here's the kicker: this was to be a temporary, six-week position. The job would actually last for the next seven years, while dominating almost every waking moment of my life.

8

YOU'RE DOING WHAT? WHERE? THE YOUNGEST WORLD'S FAIR PRESIDENT WRESTLES THE WORLD

The Furor; Pros and Cons

Knoxville was suddenly abuzz with talk of this "World's Fair." Dozens, if not hundreds, of people began exploring ideas. This was in 1975, and the city was abuzz with activity. Community curiosity was awakened, and genuine interest began to build.

Mayor Testerman set up a profusion of committees. Testerman represented the second vital link in the development of this major international event. His early and substantial commitment was vital. I can say without much disagreement that the World's Fair was not the reason he lost the mayor's race. It was not a campaign issue, at all. In fact, the effort had been resoundingly endorsed by candidate Tyree throughout the race. He never criticized or attacked the then-mayor or anybody involved in matters related to the Fair. Mayor Testerman was as supportive as one could possibly be. The community could not consider moving forward with a project this immense without the city's chief executive participating and being a vocal advocate, which Randy Tyree was as well. Mayor Tyree also secured some crucial votes later with the city council, using his influence as much as possible. Without the support of both mayors Testerman and Tyree, there would not have been a World's Fair.

King Cole, as president of Expo '74, was with the group that recruited and interviewed me to take the leadership role in Knoxville's quest, and the interview was the first time we actually met. Cole was a large, affable man who always seemed to have a positive outlook. We became good friends, and he was a willing, patient mentor as we worked our way through the rigors and layers of federal (Department of Commerce) and international (Bureau of International Exhibitions in Paris) bureaucracies.

I got involved early on with the site selection committee. We set up an office and began coordinating the efforts to bring the World's Fair to Knoxville. It was a fascinating endeavor and a sprawling, occasionally daunting, behemoth of an undertaking.

Once again, I was the youngest. As the first employee and CEO, I was the youngest president of a World's Fair.

Let me pause for a moment, and provide my list of the people crucial to the World's Fair effort, who have been and will be discussed. I want to list them:

THERE WOULD NOT HAVE BEEN A WORLD'S FAIR IN KNOX-
VILLE WITHOUT THESE PEOPLE:

W. STEWART EVANS
MAYOR KYLE TESTERMAN
JAKE BUTCHER
JIM HASLAM
KING COLE
MAYOR RANDY TYREE
BRUCE McCARTY
BILL CANNON
KNOXVILLE CITY COUNCIL
SEN. HOWARD BAKER
SEN. JIM SASSER
TN TOURISM COMMISSIONER TOM JACKSON
TOM BELL and the K.I.E.E. MANAGEMENT COMMITTEE
GOV. LAMAR ALEXANDER

THE WORLD'S FAIR WOULD NOT HAVE BEEN SUCCESSFUL
WITHOUT THESE PEOPLE:

SANDY QUINN
WALTER LAMBERT
BO'S LIFELINE: COOKIE, JACK, JON and RICK
CHARLIE SMITH
LITTON COCHRAN
ED KEEN
SANDY'S TEAM: BILL, JIM, ED and OTHERS
THE ENERGY FILLED EMPLOYEES

The contributions of these (and, obviously, many others), will become fully evident as this story unfolds.

In a shrewd organizing move for the main committee, Mayor Testerman had appointed co-chairs: Jake Butcher, head of Tennessee's then-largest bank, and Jim Haslam, the founder of the Pilot Corporation.

Jake Butcher was president and CEO of the largest bank in East Tennessee when he was appointed as chairman of the exploratory body. Later, he would become chairman of the non-profit corporation. He, too, was a young, super charismatic, and an aggressive person of note. His younger brother, C. H. Butcher, operated as a behind-the-scenes mastermind. Together, they began assembling their empire with their father's small, rural East Tennessee bank as the foundation. They both acquired banks and organized new ones. They purchased Hamilton National Bank and changed its name to United American Bank, which was the largest bank in East Tennessee and provided important support for the World's Fair. So, Butcher's involvement in leading the banking community was essential. (The Butchers' banking story alone goes from meteoric beginnings to a tragic crash at the end with both brothers eventually being incarcerated. Numerous stories and books have been written on this subject.)

Originally from Florida via Pennsylvania, Jim Haslam, fresh from being a star player at St. Pete High School (FL), arrived in Knoxville as a UT football recruit. He later became a starter on the offensive line of General Robert Neyland's 1951 championship team, and served as a team captain in 1952. Haslam was the founder of the Pilot Oil Corporation, which has since become Pilot Flying J, the largest travel center chain in the country. Haslam's youngest son, Bill, is a former mayor of Knoxville and former governor of Tennessee, while his oldest son, Jimmy, is now the Chairman of Pilot Flying J and the owner of the NFL team, the Cleveland Browns, with his wife, Dee. They are also co-owners of the major league soccer team, the Columbus Crew (Columbus, OH).

I met Haslam through Howard Baker, and even though we're from different sides of the political aisle, we worked together on various things dealing with the University of Tennessee. The questions he would always ask were these: "What's best for the University of Tennessee? What's best for the city of Knoxville? What's best for the state of Tennessee? What do we have to do to achieve those things?"

Haslam and his delightful wife, Natalie, hosted several functions related to the World's Fair, particularly for President Ronald Reagan following the Fair's Opening Day ceremony. The arrangement that Haslam and I had was the epitome of bipartisanship: people working in tandem on both sides of the aisle. It was totally necessary; we could not have survived without Haslam's vital input, involvement, and commitment. He was a yeoman, fully present every step of the way.

Haslam was vice chairman on the Knoxville International Energy Exposition board, and took over as chairman for most of 1978 while Butcher was running for governor. When Butcher was defeated, Haslam supported his return to the board.

When I was being interviewed by Butcher, Haslam, King Cole, and others about joining the staff and heading up the K.I.E.E, I asked

Butcher a question. It appeared that he was planning on running for governor again in 1978, two years after I would have come on board, so, I asked him a question: What was more important, being governor or the World's Fair? He said that the World's Fair was more important and that he would never do anything to hurt the effort toward the Fair. That was important for me to know.

Butcher was an enigmatic figure. He married a knockout beauty, former actress Sonya Wilde, who gave up her career in Hollywood to return to Tennessee, to marry Butcher and start raising a family. They built an immense mansion overlooking Melton Hill Lake in Clinton (Anderson County) that they christened, "Whirlwind." They hosted scores of events related to the World's Fair, entertaining hundreds of assorted groups from across the spectrum of supporters, both before and throughout the Fair's 184 days. Through his business connections, Butcher was instrumental in bringing the country of Peru to the World's Fair. I could go on and on about the contributions that members of the Butcher family made to the exposition.

Butcher put a lot of effort into the World's Fair. He was completely enthusiastic and supportive. We never had a disagreeable word; though we may have disagreed about some things on occasion, as I did with other members of the board, we always agreed on the outcome. At all times throughout the World's Fair, during its development and execution, Butcher never asked me to do anything that even hinted of impropriety, nor expected me to do anything off-color. I bring that up because later the Butcher banks had difficulties. They actually went under right after the World's Fair. Yet, he was a strong supporter who became a good friend, and we continued to be friends until he died in

2017. Without him, his leadership, and his bank's commitment, we would not have had a World's Fair.

Back to developing the Fair: We had to get first-round approval from our own government (through the U.S. Department of Commerce), prior to submitting an application to the Bureau of International Expositions (BIE), the governing body of World's Fairs, headquartered in Paris. Those were the first official tasks, but another concurrent task we had was informing local stakeholders and quickly harnessing their enthusiasm and mobilizing their support.

Because the World's Fair "label" sounded so BIG to some, we reframed it as an International Energy Exposition (Energy Expo '82), which brought a comfort level to many important supporters. A Special Category exhibition limits the types of programs to those focusing on the theme of the six-month event. Another significant difference is that the buildings constructed for international participants are temporary, and are leased to the countries by the Fair organizer.

In contrast, General Category Exhibitions, such as the one in Montreal in 1968, utilize permanent buildings constructed and directly paid for by the participant nations. Spokane '74 was a Special Category exhibition with the theme of the environment, while Knoxville's Special Category exhibition derived its energy theme from its proximity to the Tennessee Valley Authority's massive, hydroelectric power-producing dam operation and the Oak Ridge National Lab's experimentation with high-level, and sometimes controversial, alternative forms of power.

We needed an outlet for all the volunteers who wanted to be a part of the development in Knoxville, so we established "Expo Energizers," a group of dedicated people who volunteered their time to be of service and help with logistics. They truly exemplified the "energy" which we so desperately needed early on to keep the sizzle alive.

We also needed an interim funding source, so we set up a mechanism to finance the application process, and to facilitate all that needed to transpire for approval. As there was no GoFundMe.com at that time, six of Knoxville's seven local banks created a consortium which enabled individuals to become "Expo Ambassadors" by signing a promissory note for a thousand dollars. Those notes provided the operational dollars to generate revenue to fund initial construction and management costs. If we were successful, the "Ambassadors'" notes would be folded into the overall financing of the Expo, and the 1000 signatories would not be called upon to make good on their commitments. I'm happy to report that not a single note had to be repaid.

We then had to convince the Department of Commerce that Knoxville had the ability and the capacity to host an international exhibition. We assembled an impressive package of stakeholder commitments, funding sources and verifiable statistical information in our effort to persuade the somewhat-skeptical U.S. government officials that we had a credible plan, backed by a team of seasoned experts. We engaged Economics Research Associates (ERA) of Los Angeles, the nation's foremost feasibility firm and a specialist in major tourist attraction studies, to review and assess our preliminary assumptions and financial forecasts. While expensive, the company's final report served as a solid stamp of credibility. (Then and now, these firms have as much or more to lose as their clients do in the long run......so, it behooves them to get it right, whether it reinforces the client's desired outcome or not.) The ERA report provided a serious, in-depth analysis, conducted by consummate professionals, while doubling as a formidable road map for achieving success.

To the eternal disappointment of the legions of Fair naysayers, Knoxville enjoyed two positive, unchangeable, undeniable, defining factors: it was within a day's drive of 50 million Americans, and, equally important, it was less than 40 miles away from the Great Smoky Mountains National Park—the nation's most visited, a fact which often goes unheralded. Based on the Park's more than nine million annual visits (a figure that rose to 14.1 million visits in 2021), ERA's modeling projected that the Fair could reasonably expect more than 11 million visits during its six-month run, from May 1st through October 31st. So, we only needed an average of 63,000 visitors during the Fair's 184 days. That was do-able, right?

Also essential was the support of our local and state communities, including business and political leadership. Knoxville's initial application came while Gerald Ford was president. Ford had replaced President Richard Nixon after the disastrous Watergate scandal led to Nixon's resignation. In 1976, Jimmy Carter was elected president, and several on our board had close associations with the former Georgia governor. Jake Butcher was one of the leading national fundraisers for the new president-elect, and was very active in the Democratic Party at the state level. He was a major fundraiser for our first-term Senator-elect Jim Sasser, a Democrat replacing Republican Bill Brock. Historically, the legislature had been Democratic, and Butcher had backed many of those politicians.

Senator Sasser was a young, adroit new senator, who was supportive of the World's Fair from Day One. Literally. From the day he was sworn in at the Senate in January of 1977, he began supporting us.

Senator Baker had been a friend of mine and, obviously, of many in the community. He was from the Knoxville area, and his venerable law firm was headquartered in Knoxville. Both were 100% in our court from the beginning. As a Republican majority leader, Senator Baker could not have been more genial or helpful. When Pres. Carter lost his re-election bid to Ronald Reagan; Baker's relationship with him, both politically and personally, saved the day. President Reagan and his administration could have abandoned the World's Fair by not supporting an effort led by Pres. Carter. I cannot overemphasize the importance of their political and personal involvement.

That was also true of the members of Tennessee's congressional delegation. Rep. John Duncan, a longtime Republican congressman from Knoxville, who was also a former mayor of the city, was extremely supportive, as were the balance of the Democrats and Republicans in the nine-member delegation. Longtime congressman, Rep. Harold Ford, Sr. of Memphis, was helpful in persuading the liberal caucus. It was fun watching him work to gain their support for our appropriation.

The congressman from Nashville, Rep. Bill Boner, who later became mayor of Music City, was encouraged by Tom Jackson to start the first-ever Tourism Caucus in Congress. As chairman, Boner's support was significant and appreciated.

Jackson was the first Commissioner of Tourist Development, a position created during Gov. Blanton's term. His support was obviously important and mutually beneficial—the World's Fair would be a boon to tourism in Knoxville and the state. More importantly, however, Jackson's support enabled us to neutralize what could have easily been, not only a lack of support, but, perhaps, even overt opposition from Gov. Blanton.

Here's the backstory. One of Blanton's opponents in the 1974 primary was Jake Butcher, one of six opponents to whom he wasn't close. He had no particular ties with Randy Tyree, the new Democratic mayor of Knoxville. I had known Blanton when he was a congressman and I was in the governor's office, and we had several mutual friends, and always seemed to get along.

I had a cousin, Jim Howell, a professional printer with a master's degree in printing from Syracuse University. His wasn't a common skill set, and he was between jobs, so I arranged for him to have an interview for a state job during the Ellington administration. They hired him to run state printing, a non-political job. As far as I knew, Howell had performed admirably in the position.

When Blanton took office, Howell called me and said he heard he was about to be fired. I offered to check on that and contacted a friend in the governor's office. I explained the situation, adding that I didn't even know Howell's political affiliation but that he seemed to be doing a solid, apolitical job with the printing.

My friend said it certainly shouldn't be a problem and he would talk with the governor and get back with me. He called me back in 10 minutes and said we did, in fact, have a problem. He told the governor the situation, and the governor said, "F--k Bo Roberts." At that point, I realized that I wasn't able to be of assistance and told my cousin to get his resume in order.

Blanton had unsuccessfully run for Senate against Howard Baker, a known friend of mine even if I wasn't involved in his campaign. (Hell, I may have even voted for Baker in that election.) Apparently, Gov. Blanton saw me as a rival, supporting his past political opponents.

Just as the support of Knoxville's mayor was essential to the World's Fair, so was support from the state. Blanton could have been an implacable roadblock, if not for the work of Tom Jackson. We didn't explicitly characterize it this way, but basically, Jackson neutralized the governor and kept him kind of away from what was going on with the World's Fair development. Jackson was very supportive in other ways, too, but without him in that particular position, we would not have been able to have the World's Fair.

Finally, there was Gov. Lamar Alexander: without his support and bipartisanship, the World's Fair would not have occurred. I had known him going back to the Ellington years, during the transition when he was on Senator Baker's staff. He worked on the transition for Gov. Dunn, and I urged him to become part of the administration. He said no, he had other things to do. Little did I know that he would later run for governor.

Alexander had lost the gubernatorial election in 1974 when he ran against Ray Blanton, a Democrat. In the post-Watergate years, most any Democrat would triumph. Now, Alexander was running again.

Well before the primaries of the statewide governor's race in early 1978, a mutual friend of Jim Haslam's arranged a breakfast meeting in Knoxville between myself and Alexander, who hailed from nearby Maryville. We spent a few hours reviewing the Fair's development. Obviously, he knew that Butcher was running in the Democratic primary. He suggested that if Butcher were not the Democratic nominee that he could be more helpful as governor than Bob Clement (whom Butcher eventually defeated in the Democratic primary).

So, Alexander was the Republican nominee, running against the Democratic nominee, who was the chairman of the corporation sponsoring the World's Fair. Yet, the World's Fair was never an issue during either the gubernatorial campaign or the Knoxville mayoral campaign. To Alexander's credit, he could have attacked Butcher based on his World's Fair chairmanship as a powerful banker representing "big money," which would have been an interesting tactic for a Republican to take against a Democrat. But, he didn't.

Governor Alexander assumed office in January of 1979. Without his support, we would not have had the World's Fair, and we certainly would not have received the interstate infrastructure improvements that were so sorely needed. Gov. Alexander appointed Bill Sansom, one of our board members, as his Commissioner of Transportation and head of highway development. Sansom was a no-nonsense man who was well-acquainted with Knoxville's downtown interstate challenges and its other issues. His crucial support may have come later in terms of chronology, but it was equally as important as the contributions made by many others named here.

In addition to the interstate improvements, there were a myriad of other commitments and support we had to have from the Fair's home state. Gov. Alexander and his administration were stalwarts in providing the needed assistance. One of my vivid memories during the Fair was our governor, a talented pianist, performing with the Knoxville Symphony in the State of Tennessee Ampitheatre in a white tuxedo!

With so much business and political support coalescing around us, we continued working with the Department of Commerce professionals to seek approval for Knoxville. Initially, we had applied for an event to be held in 1980. We quickly realized that we needed additional lead time and moved our date to 1982. New Orleans had also applied for an international exposition in 1982, as well. Due to our head start, their approval date was moved to 1984.

We were successful in getting the recommendations from the Department of Commerce to proceed with the theme of "Energy Turns the World." Why energy as a theme? Partly because our nation and the world was in an oil and gasoline crisis. It was a sign of the times that the 1970s saw interstate speeds lowered to 55 miles an hour to conserve gas. Gas lines were everywhere; demand, of course, raised prices. Oil had been embargoed by the Middle East, and gas prices soared. Inflation was outta sight. At that time, people realized that something had to change, not just for gas for cars, but for energy itself. It was going to take more than the traditional coal and petrol from the ground to provide energy for the country and the world. So, we chose energy as the theme with a goal of exploring innovations in solar power and other things that would come.

Energy was a natural strength in our area with the hydropower-initiated Tennessee Valley Authority as the largest public utility in the world, the work by Union Carbide for the Oak Ridge National Laboratory, and research done at UT. Our area had the credibility to address energy issues on a world stage. Walter Lambert, who had managed federal affairs for me at UT, took a leave of absence to become the "energy guy," and he assembled world leaders in energy for three international symposia. Impressive forums were assembled in October of 1980, November of 1981, and the final gathering of the leading scientists from the participating countries, May 24-27, 1982. Papers were issued, among the conclusions was appreciation to Fair for creating a forum that focused on the "new agenda" item of energy as a field, a challenge and opportunities. After the conclusion of the synopsis, Lamber was recruited once again and he skillfully accomplished other essential tasks for the Fair, and set up and managed the committee to redevelop the Fair site.

Related to energy, Litton Cochran's contribution to the World's Fair was one of the largest, literally. One of the first people to franchise McDonald's locations in East Tennessee, Cochran envisioned our symbolic structure, the Sunsphere. A few years before the Fair, he sensibly thought that we needed an architectural statement piece, an edifice that announced, loud and clear: "This is the World's Fair. This is Energy." With the sun being the ultimate purveyor of energy, Litton worked with that idea. He had worked with Community Tectonics,

Hubert Bebb's architectural firm in Gatlinburg. (Because of Gatlinburg's strict design codes, Litton used them to design McDonald's locations to conform with local guidelines.) Bebb then presented Litton with an early sketch of what would become the Sunsphere. It was to be our version of Seattle's Space Needle or San Antonio's Hemisfair, a lasting city symbol. Anybody who comes to Knoxville can't help but see the Sunsphere, still standing as a monument to the World's Fair and Litton's vision, determination, and investment.

Then began several meetings in Paris (which was a pleasant duty, more on that later), and on April 27, 1977, we received the official sanction and agreement from the Bureau of International Expositions to move forward. It was an exceptional day. Our delegation included Mayor Tyree and several members of the K.I.E.E. board of directors. We set up a live announcement in Knoxville with a phone call and had a televised program from Paris, which kicked-off a round of exhilarating celebrations. Knoxville, little ol' Knoxville, had been approved to go ahead with its outrageous ideas, wild aspirations, and dreams. It was a milestone day in the history of travel and tourism in Knoxville and in the state of Tennessee.

As much fun as the celebration was, I knew the work had only just begun and that the BIE had actually given us an expensive hunting license. Unlike many other countries, expositions are not fully funded by the government. The government participates, yes. The U.S. would build its own pavilion, provide the diplomatic staffing and some general support, but the host committee had the responsibility to finance the exposition itself.

In addition, to make the event feasible, there were major infrastructure problems that had to be addressed. A few feet from the exposition's site loomed an infamous intersection known nationwide as "Malfunction Junction," where I-75 and I-40 intersected (or collided) into one lane right in the middle of downtown Knoxville. Think about it: one of the nation's major North–South routes crossed with the nation's East–West route, with a single access lane. Seriously? During the summertime, there would be horrific traffic jams, with cars backed up for 60 miles, all the way to the Kentucky border.

Already a national embarrassment, now we were proposing to add 11 million visitors over six months to this intolerable mix? We had to have massive funding from the state and federal governments and strong support to make all this happen. And, by "support," I mean political, bureaucratic, engineering, and guts. I often said that a special event, especially one this major, "takes the 'what we need' wishes off the shelf and places a deadline." We would need more than a billion dollars of road improvements and had to have it completed in less than five years.

Then our own "hunting license" amounted to an estimated $250 million that we had to finance in the hope that we could open and generate enough funds from sponsors and visitors to pay everything off. I had earlier mentioned the economic study done by ERA (Economic Research Associates) that projected it was possible to have 11.1 million visitors during the six-month fair, generating enough revenue to finance the project. And, if anything were left over, it would come back to the community because we were a non-profit organization.

As we were developing the fair, we had contacts with national media for print and television interviews. A reporter from *The Wall Street Journal* interviewed me once, and I could tell by her line of questioning (and my own newspaper experience) that her story would have a patronizing tone. I don't recall her name, but she'll live on in infamy forever. Forty years later people still mention it as though it was just last week. The resulting article, titled, "What If You Gave a World's Fair and Nobody Came?" began with this line, "This scruffy little city on the banks of the Tennessee River is trying to put together an international event . . ." To be fair, I don't think she got any facts wrong, but it was mostly her opinion, deriding our efforts at urban renewal and comparing our efforts to the movie, *The Producers*, wherein a Broadway producer purposefully stages a flop to bilk investors (incidentally, also one of my favorite movies).

The "scruffy little city" line stuck. It became a rallying cry. Our attitude was that we in the Knoxville family can criticize ourselves but we'll be damned if some New Yorker is going to come down and disparage us. We already had terrific support, but that article generated even more and galvanized the community into making sure the Fair succeeded. That "scruffy little city" label would return at opportune moments.

Another media memory came from a reporter from a regional news service. He fired off question after question, eventually asking me what I would do if WWIII broke out during the Fair.

I paused, waiting to see if he was serious. I told him I didn't know—we hadn't made any precise preparations for what we would do in such a situation in the nuclear-war-nervous 1980s. I didn't have time to think about WWIII. I had to get ready for the World's Fair.

The questions kept coming: "You're doing a what *where*?"

"Yes, we're doing a World's Fair in Knoxville." And, we began marketing it.

Vital Local Support

One of the conditions of getting a project like ours approved, first by the Federal officials and then internationally, was, obviously, local support. That's why Mayor Testerman's initial actions were so important to get the idea seriously considered, and with the unexpected change in the mayor's office, Randy Tyree became a critical cog in the effort to gain approval. Mayor Tyree could not have been more supportive. While he and I got along great, he also worked shoulder-to-shoulder with many members of our Board of Directors, who had not supported him. His commitment wasn't just a sort of ho-hum, lackluster, passive support; he was "all in," as we say in politics. Evidence of that was his leadership in working with Knoxville's City Council, whose direct support in approving a $11.6 million bond issue to purchase the site was the real "make or break" moment. We all worked exceptionally hard to accomplish this, but no one worked harder or took more public leadership than Mayor Tyree. The vote was 5-2 with two abstentions. The "heroes" to us (villains to some!) were Tee Bellah, Rex Davis, Theotis Robinson, Jack Sharp and Jean Teague. Voting against were Arthur "Smiley" Blanchard, and passing (not voting) were Mrs. W.B. Hembree and Mrs. Bernice O'Connor.

Without them, and without their stellar continued support and leadership, the 1982 World's Fair would not have been. There were several other attempts to hold a referendum on the bond issue but the same stalwarts, occasionally joined by one or two of the dissenting members, voted those efforts down as well. I felt if we had a referendum we could have won, but the time, effort and resources that would have dangerously altered our very tight schedule.

Get Real, Get Money

In the meantime, we were putting together the financing package. We set about getting bids from investment bankers to create a funding plan. First Boston Corporation was the lead investment bank. They developed a plan that involved three tiers of banks throughout the country, with Chemical Bank in New York as the lead bank in a consortium of national, regional, and local banks. Essentially—not to get too far in the weeds on this—it said local banks would put the first money in but take the last money out. Then the regional banks like Wachovia and other banks in the Southeast region would put up the second tier, and they would have the second money out.

And, putting the last money in, which would be the largest amount and the first money to be repaid, would be the national banks. Much of the largest amount would come from national banks, led by Chemical Bank. They would get the first money out, which would be pretty much guaranteed if the World's Fair opened. They were secure in their loan, but everybody was at risk based on projections, their faith in Knoxville and Tennessee, and our ability to do something that had never been done before in the Southeast.

That day in October 1979 was the day I always said that the Fair finally felt real—when we closed the loan for $30 million at Chemical Bank in New York. The loan gave us the resources to move ahead, and to the financial world, we were "real."

Bob Worthington, general counsel for the Fair, and a member of the Management Committee and Board, was with me at that meeting. He was a valuable asset and tireless supporter, putting people and opportunities together to make things happen. (He was a partner in the law firm of Baker, Worthington, Crossley, Stansberry & Woolf. Worthington was the Democrat who partnered with GOP leader Sen. Howard Baker).

The bank went over all the projections and determined that they would do better than break even and would come within a million dollars of their target return. I said, "That's close enough; let's sign the paperwork." Worthington said, "Time out, everybody." He produced a cigar from his pocket (this was when people still smoked in offices). Leaning back and lighting up, he continued, "I've been waiting all my life to be involved in a deal where 'within a million dollars or so' is close enough."

Though not many people would recognize his name, nonetheless, Worthington had to sign off on the legality of the documents, and he was also an essential element in the Fair's overall success.

The senior Chemical Bank official, Tom O'Brien, who came to Knoxville during the Fair to manage the banks and the loan, had this to say when I talked to him during my research for this book: "I don't think the Fair ever appreciated what it had accomplished with that bank agreement. To the best of my recollection, it had never been done before or since, at least within the USA. I mean 24 banks tiered by region, last in first out, etc. and everyone got paid. Amazing!."

An interesting side note for those interested in finance: the prime rate was steep then, well beyond the normal level of 6%. For our financing package, Chemical Bank, in a worst case scenario, projected that prime might reach 13%. Our loan was 2.5 points over prime, so the worst we could possibly pay in interest was 15.5%.

Think about that today. The prime rate is usually in the 2–3% range. Well, they were a bit off with their projections. The prime rate actually peaked at 21% which meant that we were paying 23.5%. So, any money we took in early meant a lot more to us than the money we received later (advance ticket sales, sponsorships, etc.). The only major over-budget item was, in the final accounting and analysis, interest costs...we were more than $5 million beyond the amount budgeted in this category, money that would have been turned over to the community at the end of the Fair, if the interest rate crisis hadn't occurred.

Maybe the Shortest Out-of-Work Period in History

A few years before the Fair, we were still raising money locally, with people signing notes for which they would be 100% liable. After the executive committee meetings in the conference room of one of the participating banks, we were scheduled to hold one of our typical rallies in the lobby to get our supporters fired up to raise more money.

In one of those executive committee meetings, someone brought up the idea of getting new leadership, some sort of national name to be president of the World's Fair. I was blindsided. The committee essentially handed me my walking papers.

The meeting adjourned, but I realized I still had to lead a rally for 300 people in the lobby. I made a decision. I jumped up on a desk and went for it. I delivered a spirited pitch, my 'Sermon on the Mount' for the World's Fair. It seemed to work. We raised a lot of money that night.

Afterward, one of the board members, a friend, told me to forget about what had happened upstairs. I don't know how much my speech factored in, but I didn't do it to save my job. I was speaking from the heart, in the moment. Hell, I was committed to the World's Fair. I may have thought about telling the Board to "Go F... yourself," but I didn't. So, for a short time that night, I was fired, then rehired—all without missing a paycheck.

I was too busy to spend time trying to see what and who all led that action. I decided not to waste my time worrying about it. If what I was doing wasn't good enough, then so be it.

How (Not) to Buy a Railroad

Very early in the process, the site selection committee (of which I was a member, appointed by Mayor Testerman), considered a variety of sites. If we were going to do a World's Fair, the easiest thing to do would be to go out in the countryside, find a couple hundred vacant acres (relatively flat), then come in and build for the event. Easy construction, easier parking and access, etc. But, after the party, what would be left of any value or permanent use? We began seriously looking into the downtown area.

We looked at one of the worst areas in downtown, which was the virtually abandoned L & N and Southern Railways site. What could it be that would benefit the city of Knoxville? Obviously, anything would have been an improvement over that 70+ acres of a pitiful-looking ditch that separated downtown Knoxville from the UT campus and the Fort Sanders neighborhood. So, that was the site our committee recommended.

So, to complete the World's Fair site, we dealt with two railroads. The bulk of the site was owned by L&N, which was not operating and had abandoned its tracks. We ended up turning the large, ornate passenger station (remember when railroads carried passengers?) into a functioning building, which later included my office, restaurants, and retail outlets. It's still in use for various functions to this day. The second railroad, Southern Railway, headquartered in Washington D.C., was operating one freight train a day. We purchased various pieces of Southern property in and near our site. Most of those pieces were then purchased from us by UT, which would take possession after the World's Fair. It was a good deal for everyone.

Dealing with the Southern Railway was an interesting experience. I traveled to their headquarters, located in a nondescript old building. I noticed something different upon entering their offices—there were very few women. I recalled the railroad executive culture, which included traveling with their secretaries, and it was untoward for them to travel with females, so that's why the clerical staff was mostly older men, many wearing green eyeshades. I found that dealing with Southern Railway also revealed other rather antiquated business practices, as well. It took some interesting conversations, but over a period of time we worked it out to get the arrangements we needed. They agreed to operate one train a day, between the hours of 11 p.m. and 7 a.m., so there was no interference with our 10 a.m.–10 p.m. operating hours.

The city of Knoxville had bought most of the property, but we still had to acquire some of the L&N property. including the station. I had been negotiating at their headquarters in Louisville with their president, Prime F. Osborne III, a very nice guy. I happened to be in my office one Saturday morning when I got a call from Osborne. He said, "I hate to bother you on a weekend, but I've got a dilemma, and I want to see if we can get it worked out." He told me there'd been a delegation of businesspeople from Knoxville who were trying to take over a part of the World's Fair. They saw an opportunity and went to Louisville and made offers to buy the property out from under us. I don't know exactly what was offered, but it was more than we had discussed.

Osborne said he wanted to honor his word and honor our agreement. So, we worked it out: I verbally agreed at that moment and sent a telegram confirming that we would purchase the property for $2.5 million. That was the good news. The bad news was that we, the K.I.E.E. Corporation, had about $30,000 in the bank. I obviously had some confidence that we would be able to provide the money, which we did when our loan closed later that year. That was among the many limbs that I willingly went out on during the development of the Fair.

I really appreciated this gentleman, Osborne, standing by his word. As head of a large, publicly traded corporation, he could have been criticized for accepting less money than he was offered for the property. But, his word mattered more than the money....you don't encounter that many of those in this life.

Seeing is, Undoubtedly, Believing

The first year of construction basically consisted of underground infrastructure work: Tearing down and installing the utilities, altering the flow of Second Creek, and demolishing the buildings that needed to be removed. We had to get the tracks taken up and one reinstalled. And then, in the spring of 1980, when that first steel beam came out of the ground, suddenly people in Knoxville began to realize that this event was actually going to be real.

Thanks to that crucial financing, we were able to develop 74 acres of a wonderful playground on which the world could come and be completely and wholly entertained.

Unsecured Creditors: Bruce McCarty and Bill Cannon

Bruce McCarty was the lead architect of the firm McCarty, Bullock, and Holsaple, which bid for and were selected as lead architects. They were also associated with various international firms which had some experience in these areas. I had known McCarty for several years and had mostly been involved with him in business projects, such as Cherokee Bluffs, which his firm designed.

He is one of the most high-caliber, high-quality people I've ever known. I'm a great admirer of his architectural work. He also had a great eye for talent. His firm was very selective, and being hired by them was a high honor; one they bestowed upon Bob Church, whom I worked with in developing UT's architecture school. McCarty and his firm put their reputation on the line with the World's Fair, and they put in tremendous hours to make it work.

Closely allied with McCarty and his company was Bill Cannon, the principal in the Nashville-based engineering company Barge, Waggoner, Sumner and Cannon (now known as the Barge Company). Cannon became an even more valuable asset later, when we were working with the Department of Transportation in redesigning the interstates. He conceived of some especially innovative ideas there.

There was no guarantee that McCarty and Cannon would be receiving any remuneration until we closed our final loan in 1979. Early on, they were attending a meeting that I'd set up with a government official from the Department of Commerce. Eventually, the official looked at them and asked McCarty, "What's your position?" McCarty answered, "Unsecured creditor."

That's the way I've described them both—unsecured creditors. Their commitment was very real and very expensive. There were no two people with more concrete, money, or time invested than Bruce McCarty and Bill Cannon—it would have been a huge loss for them both if the Fair had not come to fruition. They constructed a model of the Fair site that I took to New York to showcase during television interviews and then took it to Paris, as well, in order to present it to the officials at the BIE. It was an exceptionally effective (albeit expensive) sales tool.

So, without Cannon and McCarty's commitment, time, involvement, and, perhaps most importantly, trust, the World's Fair would not have happened. We couldn't have waited until 1979 to start designing the site; we'd already begun some demolition utilizing the money that the city had committed. It was a huge leap of faith for both of them. I've always been indebted to them, as really the people of Knoxville and the world would be, too, if they'd had any knowledge of the extent of their phenomenal contributions.

The Overseas Trips: Selling the World, Seeing the World and Convincing the World to Come to Knoxville

All countries with which the U.S. had official relations were invited to participate in our sanctioned international exhibition by U.S. Secretary of State Cyrus Vance on behalf of our government.

Nothing would happen automatically; we knew we had to persuade countries to be a part of our event in Knoxville. Our U.S. government was eager to have our friends participate, but not to the extensive degree that we were—it was the private money in our non-profit endeavor that was at risk. We knew that if we did not have a good number and mix of foreign nations involved, we would not have a successful World's Fair.

We needed to secure "headliner" participants to announce early on, which would create the necessary credibility and momentum for locking down commitments from other nations. Our early targets were our neighbors, Canada and Mexico, and then our European allies. Utilizing King Cole's contacts, we began working directly with the officials we knew in the Canadian government, as well as government and energy officials in Mexico. We were able to get their commitments officially announced, while finalizing the specifics regarding the size and scope of their participation.

An interesting dynamic developed with our European allies, who, like many countries in the world, were facing tough economic times. The idea began to develop about the newly formed European Union having a joint participation with each of their nine countries having individual exhibitions within the European pavilion. After many meetings, we were able to work out an exciting agreement, and when we were able to announce it, we immediately had the additional nine nations as part of our portfolio.

Another early focus was our strong ally, Japan. I made many trips to meet with the officials in Japan, and I found their culture extremely interesting, exceedingly polite and accommodating, yet reserved. They knew, and I knew that they were going to participate, but they're also precise in their ways, following a diplomatic and bureaucratic timeline that was far slower than that to which I was accustomed. We were anxious to get them to go ahead and commit. We knew they were going to be a part of the Fair as a major exhibitor, and, as with any marketing situation, we wanted to add to the momentum as soon as possible.

Still, we had to take it step-by-step. With each visit, the size of the audience got larger and larger. At the final meeting with the absolute top person in their government/business coalition, I finally officially learned that Japan would participate. Two billion yen had been allocated for its presentation (I remember sitting there trying as quickly as I could to convert that number into dollars, finally realizing that it was about $20 million). It was a wonderfully happy time when later that day I was able to Telex our office in Knoxville to relay the grand announcement that Japan was "in" and to go ahead and release the story.

Our major target, and "anchor tenant" for sure, was the Soviet Union. We had been working with them from the very beginning. The Soviet Union was one of the signature attractions at King Cole's Spokane World's Fair in 1974. Their lead guys became good friends, and there was no doubt they were going to be a major part of our event. I made three official visits to the Soviet Union, where I was treated royally.

Moscow was a somewhat drab city, but I was able to attend the Bolshoi Ballet and to visit other great cultural sites while I was there. However, I think I was most struck by the number of monuments and statues commemorating different events during WWII. There, and in other places that I visited in the Soviet Union, I was surprised by what I called the "Omnipresence of World War II." This was in the late 1970s, not that long after the war. As a comparison, the U.S. lost more than 400,000 people in the war, but the Soviet Union had more than 10 million casualties. The gold stars I saw in the windows of family homes in the U.S. made a huge impression on me as a kid, so I fully understood the enormity of the impact that war had on Russia and what became their satellite countries.

A trip I made to St. Petersburg was also quite awe-inspiring. We talked a lot about the "900-day Siege," since I'd read many books about it during my discovery of my abiding interest in history. I was there once on what they call the "White Nights," a shifting period of time in the late spring/early summer, which peaks on June 22nd, the longest day of the year. Due to its northern latitude, St. Petersburg doesn't experience complete darkness during this time. My wife and I went out with one of our guides. I've never seen so many publicly inebriated Russians. Normally very deferential, yet reserved around Westerners, on this night, they were beyond friendly and much more receptive to conversation. As it's no longer the Soviet Union, I suspect those White Nights are even wackier now than they were in the past. I was delighted to visit the Grand Peterhof Palace, where I saw, with my own eyes, the extraordinary treasures that I had read so much about. I imagined the Russians, who, despite their starvation, had so meticulously preserved and buried those magnificent objects in advance of the predicted Nazi invasion.

I thought even more about the dichotomy between a Communist system which rejected the monarchical system, while so devotedly protecting the treasures of a dynasty that they concluded by execution. It makes so little sense. Regardless, for us and the generations to come, thank goodness, that they erred on the side of preservation.

During one of my first trips to Russia, they assigned a young man to me to be my guide and assistant primarily for translation purposes. Once at the end of breakfast, Sasha asked how I liked it, and I gave the "OK" sign, curling my forefinger and thumb together. We repeated this exchange every morning for a few days until Sasha finally asked me, in his soft, British-like accent, "Bo, do Americans make signs with their hands?" I replied in the affirmative and demonstrated a few, like "timeout." He asked if some were "injurious or insulting to another person." I said "yes," and went on to explain the classic American middle finger. He politely explained that our "OK" symbol is basically the same as giving someone the middle finger in Russia. I was appalled when I realized that for the past few days I'd been answering polite questions with the equivalent of a "F--k you!" Thankfully, Sasha understood my most innocent mistake. A tip for international travelers: Hand gestures don't always translate. Another lesson learned.

I made a side trip to Kiev (now Kyiv), Ukraine, south of Russia proper but a part of the Soviet Union, where it seemed as though the people were less reserved and a bit friendlier. On a brisk boat ride on the Dnieper River, my hosts took me to a high bank above the river to see a statue of a WWII soldier. In the short time I was there, I saw several wedding parties approach the statue and throw flowers into the river from there as part of the ceremony, an acknowledgment to all of those who had lost their lives during World War II. I also realized that when I was in Kiev that it had essentially been totally rebuilt because it was almost virtually destroyed during the war. The citizens, who rebuilt it from memories and photographs, did an exceptional job in their efforts to replicate their stunning city.

Traveling with the King

King Cole and I traveled thousands of miles together throughout the world and had plenty of time to talk, plan, laugh, and enjoy as well.

One of the ways he influenced me was in helping me become knowledgeable and appreciative of wine, and to grasp the additional pleasure that it adds to the joy of living. Since much of our travel was centered in Paris, we were able to practice Wine Appreciation 101 a lot! During a rare weekend off, he took me to explore France's Burgundy region and opened my eyes and palate to the wonders of pinot noir. One of the fun tidbits from that jaunt was this: While barrel tasting a noted pinot, the winemaker said the region's favorite expression was this: "I don't remember the place, nor do I remember the girl, but the wine was Chambertin!" That gave me a perspective about the exalted place that wine holds with the French populace. I digress, but Cole provided me with a gift that, to this day, is one of the most enjoyable parts of my everyday life. The more I learn about wine, the more I know how much more there is to learn. Cheers to my late friend, King Cole.

The love of and appreciation of wine came in handy many times as I entertained, hosted, visited, and sought commitments of government leaders across many continents. Again, Cole's experience and personal friendships with the staff at the U.S. Department of Commerce (the first official hurdle in hosting an international exhibition), BIE staff and nation members, and individual representatives of many countries, were invaluable to our cause. I felt comfortable taking on a major task and confident in my abilities, but both levels were immeasurably accelerated by having Cole beside me as we explored a potentially impossible dream.

During those recruiting trips, I traveled primarily to Europe because we had to be in Paris to attend the all-important BIE meetings. We met there four times a year for reporting, approvals, and other parts of the labyrinth approval processes. May I say that venturing to the City of Light so frequently was never the worst part of my job.

Over the course of four years, each of my three sons made separate trips with me, representing their first visits to Europe.

My oldest son, Sam, was a senior in high school when he joined me in Paris. We took a side trip, first driving through Luxembourg's beautiful countryside and then up to Baden-Baden, Germany. He was dating a girl in high school at that time who was studying German, so he particularly enjoyed trying out his language skills with the locals. That small spa town has a famous, extraordinarily large chess board in its central park with movable, almost people-sized chess pieces. As one might imagine, it is quite an unusual and popular attraction.

We also visited Europe's oldest casino in Baden-Baden, located in an opulent Belle Epoque-style building. The 250-year-old architectural masterpiece was an eye-opening experience. Although we didn't gamble much (I'd learned my lesson at Golden Gate Park), I was struck by the number of English visitors there throwing down 5,000 mark chips (about$4,000) like they were dollar chips. We were amazed at the extravagant wealth on display. It was a James Bond-type moment, for sure.

My middle son, Andy, a rising sophomore at UT, especially liked Paris. On our side trip, we took a train to Germany, cruised up the Rhine, and journeyed over to Bonn and Berlin—making for an excellent adventure. We spent a few days in Bonn where I had a couple of meetings with German officials.

I, and I think Andy, enjoyed summer evenings outside on the town square, relaxing, eating and watching people. As I said, he had a grand ole time in Paris, especially with one young girl who was the daughter of a BIE official.

When my youngest son, Mark, made his trip with me, we had to leave Paris for a series of meetings in London. A young lady at the U.S. Embassy took a shine to him, as he was a good-looking kid (all my boys were, I say without prejudice). She said, "Let me take him," and basically kidnapped him for the better part of two days. He saw English sights I had never had the opportunity to see.

We had a wonderful time during those trips. One of the things I did with each of my sons on each of their trips was to set aside two hours for a visit to the Louvre Museum in Paris. We would see the high-lights—the *Mona Lisa*, *Venus de Milo*, and other artworks—and then explore areas that I didn't know about or would discover things to-gether because the Louvre is just so humongous and so fascinating.

One of my most unanticipated trips was to Athens, Greece. King Cole recommended a hotel and advised me to ask for a room facing the Acropolis. I arrived at night and went straight to bed without seeing anything. I got up the next morning and stepped out onto the balcony, and boom, there it was: The Acropolis. I'd seen pictures of it. I'd read about it. But, I had no concept about its size or how it so complete-ly dominates the Athens cityscape. It was an unforgettable, ethereal experience. Since my business trip ended on a Friday, I was able to escape to one of the famous Greek Islands close to Athens and relax for a few hours.

My trip to Egypt was one of the quickest trips I made anywhere. I traveled there with Jake Butcher, who had set up contacts in Cairo. On the way into and as we returned to the airport, we saw the pyramids, but there was no time to get up close. It was strictly business in Egypt. Even from a distance, the pyramids are unbelievably majestic. And, yes, Egypt decided to become a Fair participant.

People often asked me if I ever got tired of traveling. I'd say that I'd occasionally get tired *during* travel, but I never got tired *of* traveling. I'm from Harriman, Tennessee. I wasn't even sure I'd make it to Nashville, let alone around the world. I reveled in every moment of it, seeing some of the world before the world came to Knoxville.

The Russians Aren't Coming! Go Get China!

In addition to hosting our Russian friends in the U.S., we also were visited by their uber-talented architects from Czechoslovakia, who later entertained me in Prague and a Czech resort. They had already designed most of the Soviet exhibit, and it was under construction in a plant near Moscow. Our "anchor tenant" was solid, we thought; but, then things changed, unfortunately.

I have referred to politics several times—local, state, and national—but now international politics directly and dramatically impacted our efforts. In 1980, while the U.S.S.R. was building its exhibit, the Soviets invaded Afghanistan (a country America would come to know all too well decades into the future) and shook the world to its core. The 1980 Summer Olympics were slated for Moscow that year, and to sanction them and protest their aggression, President Carter announced that the U.S. would not participate (several other Western countries would also follow suit). That shook the sports world, but our world was shaken, too, because it meant that the Soviets canceled their participation in our World's Fair. Our "solid" anchor tenant was no more...also gone in one fell sweep were Czechoslovakia, Poland, and, we thought, every other Eastern European country.

Except for one.

Hungary was almost an afterthought. I made a stop there on the way somewhere else and, during a couple of days, made some appointments and some presentations. As it ended up, they accepted our invitation and became the only Eastern European participant. I was so impressed by Hungary's independence in joining us. It's a breathtaking country, with Buda and Pest bisected by the Danube River. Their exhibit would be built around "human energy."

 At the time, the Rubik's Cube 3-D puzzle was an international sensation, and its Hungarian inventor, Ernö Rubik, visited the Fair during the Hungarian Days. He was an enormous attraction, as visitors were dying to meet him, not to mention the legions of young puzzle wizards eager to measure their puzzle-solving skills against his. While we were greatly relieved that the decision by the U.S.S.R. did not alter Hungary's commitment, it didn't alter the fact that our "star turn" anchor tenant and largest exhibitor had vanished in the metaphorical blink of an eye. (When they kept their commitment as part of the Soviet block, I couldn't help but think back to 1968 when some of Hungary's moves toward independence led to an invasion by Soviet troops that

Sec. of State Dean Rusk revealed to me and the world in a meeting before the Democratic Platform Committee in Washington D.C.).

All Hands on Deck, Target: China

Just under two years before we were due to open, we didn't have time to either feel sorry for ourselves or to wring our hands. We had to refocus and find solutions....fast. I posed the idea to my staff that we should go after the People's Republic of China (PRC). After some brief discussions and research, I presented a plan to our Board of Directors that would, hopefully, put us back on a path to success. The plan was to go all out to get the PRC. The Board and others agreed and then we had to execute.

China had been off the world radar for many years during its "cultural revolution," where the country basically disdained anything scientific or learned and went "back to the basics" of hard work and agriculture. Eventually, new leadership realized that the downward spiral wasn't going to save the world's largest country. In 1971, President Richard Nixon, in consultation with his Secretary of State, Henry Kissinger, made a strategic decision to recognize China and to accept an invitation to visit the re-emerging nation as it began awakening to the rest of the world. Part of Nixon's stroke of genius was that only a conservative Republican president would have the sort of carte blanche that didn't blink during his overtures to a Communist country. While President Nixon faced some major domestic failures soon thereafter, I believe his door-opening efforts with China were among his most important international accomplishments. It certainly changed the world.

It changed our world in Knoxville by giving us a chance to fill a major hole. We started by meeting with Tennessee's two senators, senior senator, Howard Baker and junior senator, Jim Sasser, a Democrat. Both had been strong supporters of our efforts for the World's Fair and had done everything they had been asked to do and more. Together, they got President Carter, through Secretary of State Cyrus Vance, to issue an official invitation to China to join us as a participant in 1982. Once that was accomplished, the State Department sought an invitation for us to visit with their officials to open discussions. Again, we were successful: We got the invitation, and began preparing for our visits to Beijing.

I had been planning a major trip to Australia to officially invite and negotiate terms with that great ally nation, but I had to shift immediately to focus on China. King Cole, in his invaluable way, stepped in and made that trip and the follow-up with South Korea to tie down those important nations for Knoxville. The pursuit of China, including four visits, was successful, but could not have happened without Cole's deft handling of those other, equally important commitments.

On my first trip, Chinese government officials met me at the airport, and on our trip into Beijing, I was taken aback by the traffic that consisted of at least 70% bicycles on a multi-lane highway. On all of my trips, I stayed at the Peking Hotel, interestingly keeping the pre-Revolutionary name for the city now called Beijing. The hotel, the largest I saw in the capital city, was older, and elegant in a simple way.

During my first official meeting the next morning, I presented the officials with an elaborate book prepared by my staff, with illustrations and with text written in Chinese (thanks to UT's language department). While they were reading the presentation, all of a sudden they emerged, they were confused by a statement in the presentation-that apparently projected an attendance of ELEVEN MILLION PER DAY! Needless to say, I had to calm them down, explain it was an error and go over the projections verbally through my interpreter. Lesson learned: Check and double-check everything, no matter how pressed for time.

The people I met with in China were very friendly, openly curious and seemingly excited to talk with a Westerner. I recall many times as they were driving me around Beijing, they would point out this spot or that restaurant that Sec. of State Henry Kissinger or President Richard Nixon had spoken, or given a toast, or were part of a ceremony. It was so obvious to me how much those actions and the official recognition meant to a country that was just emerging from years of darkness and withdrawal during their Cultural Revolution.

Early on, they let me know that though China had never participated in a World's Fair, they were interested but would need some help. At first, I thought they were bargaining for financial support. Over time I realized that they wanted technical assistance and professional guidance so they would not be embarrassed to be exposed to not just 11 million people, but to the world.

We were more than ready to invest and make sure that happened, because they would become our largest pavilion and most in demand, by far. I pushed for, and got, some actual bricks from the Great Wall and some of the just discovered life-size terracotta statues of warriors from the Lintong District in Xi'an. They think more than twice now about allowing those priceless objects out of the country these days, but we were lucky enough to have them showcased in Knoxville.

One episode which I think illustrates the nature of the Chinese people I encountered on my trips, came when I decided to visit Beijing's largest "department store." It was a plain, five-story building, about a block from my hotel. I wanted to buy a "Mao suit," which was an olive green or bluish-gray cotton fabric consisting of an unadorned, fatigue-like top and pants. More than 90% of the men and women wore these in public during the time I was visiting. As I walked into the store, at 6 feet tall, I was the tallest, and the only Caucasian person in the area. The people were openly curious, but totally non-threatened by my presence. I finally conveyed what I was looking for and they escorted me to the top floor. There, with the help of at least three very nice young ladies, we began the search for a suit large enough to fit me. As they worked on this, a small crowd of customers gathered around to watch. Again, openly curious with no embarrassment about being so. When they finally brought some clothes out that we thought might fit, as I held them up, the people burst into spontaneous applause. I will never forget that experience, and still regret misplacing that unattractive but historic outfit.

While our meetings went well, and we were pretty much in agreement, we couldn't seem to get it nailed down and closed. After my second trip, I had a call from a gentleman named I.E. Poon, a Chinese-American businessman who owned more than a dozen restaurants in New York City. He also happened to be a distant relative and close friend of the Chinese Premier's chief of staff. I think the majority of Mr. Poon's restaurants in New York featured Chinese cuisine, but one he operated was the Windows of the World, the swank, two-story restaurant atop the North Tower of the World Trade Center. He entertained me and we discussed how he would help us get the deal closed and he would bid on investing and running the food operations in the Chinese pavilion. (Like many thousands of others, my memories raced back to those good times as our country watched the horrors of 9-11 take place). A few days later, we flew to Beijing, had a meeting with his cousin, and within 24 hours the deal was done. Mr. Poon ultimately became the food concessionaire at the Chinese pavilion and ran a restaurant that was at total capacity for lunch and dinner for more than 180 days. He was the last piece of the "village" it took to raise the "anchor baby."

After we received the official acceptance and made a big announcement, I met the PRC's vice premier for our signing ceremony in the "Great Hall" in Tiananmen Square. That was the place that would achieve worldwide notoriety in 1989 as the striking images of "Tank Man" blocking a tank there alone during political protests circulated around the world.

A member of the K.I.E.E. Executive Committee, Jack Brennan, happened to be in that part of the world on business, so he joined me in the signing ceremony and the celebratory meal afterwards. (Side note: We didn't know each other then, but in 1967 we were two of the three Tennessee Young Men of the Year, honored by the state Jaycees.)

During the ceremony, the vice premier told me, through an interpreter, how China was looking for help with preparing for the World's

Fair. The vice premier said that because they were the most populous country, they were the lowest per capita in this category, the lowest per capita in that category. He laughed and said, "I guess it's not hard to be the lowest per capita when you've got a billion and a half people in your country."

To provide the assistance we promised, I dispatched Charlie Smith, who had joined my staff from the McCarty firm as a vice president to coordinate the onsite work of all designers and architects. He went to China to provide the professional assistance they needed. The results were fantastic, and the intense effort involving every political and business chit we had and the help from so many, to me, assured that the 1982 World's Fair was going to be successful and attract the attention and visitors we had projected.

During one of my visits, my hosts took me to visit the Great Wall, near Beijing. As we walked on the original bricks, we would lean our elbows on the surrounding sides of the wall, and I asked them if I could take just a few minutes to be by myself to absorb, observe, and just contemplate the moment.

They obliged. Allow me to share my minutes of an ethereal, thought-provoking experience here:

First, one could think about the extreme insignificance of an individual, in the sense of time (construction started some 3,000 years ago), the numbers (well over 7 billion people today, and billions more over the centuries), and the mere speck that we occupy in time and numbers. But in one speck of time and from one human being with a massive mind, thought of an idea to build a wall, and millions expanded on that idea and made it happen over the centuries since. The idea and the vision had to start with one person, and then person-by-person they determined how to build it, and brick-by-brick, millions of people built it over a three-thousand-year span.

I reflected on a similar feeling of awe when I was a 19-year-old corporal in the U.S. Air Force making my first visit to Hoover Dam outside of Las Vegas. It was the tallest dam in the U.S. and a monument to engineering. I was so pleased that after its completion in 1935 (when it was known as Boulder Dam), a plaque was produced listing the hundreds of engineers who had been a part of its construction. How proud all subsequent engineers must have been, especially those who shared the lineage. Yet, that was only a few decades ago.

As I thought about the Great Wall being the only man-made structure visible from space, the thoughts of infinitesimal existence once again crossed my mind. Thoughts of the size of the brains that first imagined that man could travel in space and those who followed and made it happen.

I kept looking down at the bricks I was walking on and those all around the massive, steep structure. I dreamed, and somehow we were able to get a few of those original bricks to be a part of China's first-ever exhibit at a World's Fair since 1904, I'm not sure what variety of reactions came from the millions of visitors who saw those in Knoxville, but I know that I will never forget my moment on the Wall.

Stateside Caviar or A Treat Fit for Kings . . . and Shahs

On one of my domestic trips I reflected on how the world changes in a short period of time. King Cole took me to the Iranian Embassy in Washington D.C. to meet the ambassador and some of the staff that he had befriended during their participation in the Spokane World's Fair. We had a delightful visit, and soon after we returned to the Hyatt Regency Hotel on Capitol Hill, I was notified we had a hand-delivered package in our names. Wrapped neatly was a pound (a freaking *pound*) of the best Iranian caviar, with a note from the ambassador saying it was compliments of the Shah of Iran. We went to our suite, ordered some good French white wine, and asked room service if they could send us some toast points, chopped onions, butter, and mayonnaise. Their curiosity got the best of them, and one asked, "Do you have some caviar in your room?" They congratulated us and brought a beautiful display. Cole and I felt obligated, because caviar has a limited window of freshness, to consume the entire pound. Yes, we felt like, well, kings.

Within months of that visit, in 1979, Iran overthrew the Shah in a revolt, and soon after, the American hostages were held captive during the last year of President Jimmy Carter's administration. Many pundits felt that this frustrating event contributed to his defeat in 1980.

Just as Cole and I had so many pleasant experiences and memories with the Russian friends who represented the U.S.S.R., world events prevented both Iran and the Soviet Union from participating in Knoxville's exposition. But, good times with a good man will always be remembered.

Tom Bell and the K.I.E.E. Management Committee

Tom Bell was chairman of the K.I.E.E. Management Committee that was formed by the Executive Committee to work with me more closely. Bell was head of the regional East Tennessee Natural Gas Association. He was a solid, thoughtful man who became a supportive friend. He gave of his time, and on several occasions, made his company helicopter available for quick trips to Nashville or to give an aerial tour of the World's Fair site to corporate or international prospects. The Management Committee had more than a dozen serious movers and shakers— the leaders, the captains of industry—in our region as members, many of whom also represented a variety of interests related to energy. We had the heads of every major employer: Alcoa, Fulton-Sylphon, the Oak Ridge National Laboratory, Union Carbide, and the president of UT. Of course, as this was the late 1970s and early 1980s, there wasn't much balance on the committee; we had one female member and one minority member. But, that's primarily how the world functioned then: The good ol' boys' network ran things.

A few months before the opening of the World's Fair, the committee decided to schedule breakfast meetings five days a week. Though it might occasionally last just 10 minutes on some days, they wanted to touch base every day. Again, these were some of the busiest people in the region, if not the country. That's how committed they were. They never interfered, but were there to help put out the figurative fires and solve problems in an open, cooperative way.

We only had one major flare up, just a few short weeks before Opening Day.

Our young, very capable Operations Director (one of the Sandy Quinn pros that he advised us to hire) was conducting a group of media members on a tour of the site, where he discussed aspects of Opening Day and the security arrangements. He then made the casual observation that perhaps local people might want to stay away on that day and come on another, less frenzied, day instead. Well, the stuff hit the proverbial fan. We went full bore, straight ahead into disaster control mode as the public reacted negatively to the media's exaggerated reporting suggesting that locals "stay home," which was not, by any stretch of the imagination, what the Operations Director was inferring. I and others assured local citizens that this was not the official Fair position, whatsoever. We went into overdrive putting out the message that everyone, particularly the area residents, who had supported and endured the years of development, were not only welcome but encouraged to be there.

Our guy, my guy, made a mistake. He was a good man, but some on the Management Committee thought he should be fired for making that statement. Never in all my time as CEO had the Board interfered with any of my personnel decisions, and I could not let it start then. I had decided, though I did not verbalize it, that if they went against my recommendation to continue his employment, then I would resign. I made my case, a motion was made to fire him, but it failed seven votes for the motion to fire, 10 against. A credit to those who didn't vote with me is that they immediately moved on to other things, and none of them expressed any animosity towards me or the situation. We took a vote, and then it was over. I was glad, however, that I didn't have to make the other decision.

Tom Jackson and the Buses

Those of us in Knoxville had been so busy getting ready for the summer of 1982 that we forgot the rest of the country was undergoing a recession. I mean, we felt the pain through our high interest rates, but the automobile industry had all but shut down due to rising energy costs. Tourism was way down.

Still, our feasibility study that told us we could draw more than 11 million people to the Fair was based on several factors. Tourism was already a major draw in the area, which was easily accessible to the eastern half of the country. The Smoky Mountains were the most visited national park in the U.S., drawing more than nine million people annually. Then there's Pigeon Forge and Gatlinburg. People going to Florida pass through here. People escaping the Florida heat come here. Typical tourism attendance is a bell curve, lower in spring and then peaking in summer when school is out, dropping again in fall, with a burst in October because of the vivid fall foliage. So, we thought attendance at the Fair would follow that projected model.

Enter Tom Jackson. The first tourism commissioner, Jackson had formed his own company, consulting on tourism around the country. He knew tour buses were one of the fastest growing segments of the tourism market.

We hired Jackson's company to pursue tour marketing and companies that had buses operating nationwide, bringing large numbers of visitors to the Smokies, Nashville, Disney World, and other attractions. They also offered package deals including hotels. The bus tour market was primarily seniors who could travel outside of the traditional tourist season. So, they were looking for attractions in April, May, early June, late August, September, and October.

Jackson and his bus outreach inverted that traditional tourism bell curve, and our attendance would be highest in May, early June, late August, September, and October.

The results were fantastic. For example, one Monday we were expecting 35,000 visitors, but 90,000 showed up. Two thirds of those people arrived on buses. One bus company operated out of Asheville, N.C., itself a gloriously beautiful destination. They would transport people to Knoxville, 90 miles away, early in the morning and return at 10 p.m., when the Fair closed. More than 90 buses a day came from Asheville alone for 180 days. Think about those numbers (that's nearly a million people). The bus companies could buy tickets in advance for a discounted price. If admission was, say, $10, the bus companies could buy tickets for $6. With interest rates so high, those upfront funds were crucial to us. When the gates opened on May 1, 1982, we knew we had pre-sold more than 6 million tickets, over half of our projected attendance.

Because of the vital support needed from the state prior to the Fair, I had listed Jackson as essential to us even having an event. His later efforts, like some others on that list, would also qualify as one who made the Fair a success.

The increased attendance would filter out to surrounding attractions, as well. Opryland in Nashville, initially concerned that the World's Fair would dampen its annual attendance, posted their highest numbers that year. A Kentucky state park near the Tennessee border found their attendance increased 540% that summer.

Jackson did even more with the group tour industry before the Fair opened.. Once, as cash flow was getting low, to the point where I might have trouble making payroll, I called Jackson for help. He reached out to the president of Greyhound, a personal friend. Jackson asked him to do three things: 1) make Greyhound the official bus line of the World's Fair, and, 2), buy $6 million in tickets, and then, 3), pay 10% upfront with a check for $600,000 the next day. Jackson flew out to Phoenix that night and returned the next day with the check. We made the payroll.

So, we ended up with thousands of buses with the largest numbers in the first and last six weeks. We would not have had that extra growth without Jackson introducing this new market. The buses became completely essential to meeting our attendance goals. That was the wonderful and vital contribution of Jackson and his team.

Jackson also led me to what was probably the best recruiting job I've ever done. That's something I admire in football coaches: The ability to invest in new talent, not only for the team's sake, but to keep their own careers alive. I didn't know it at the time, but, both my own, and the Fair's survival, would be somewhat based on meeting Sandy Quinn and utilizing his skill set, one that we needed and didn't have in Knoxville.

I was introduced to Quinn by Jackson, who told me that Quinn was speaking at a national gathering of tourism officials in Gatlinburg. He insisted that I go hear what he had to say. Quinn had worked for a little company called Disney, where he was one of a small group of key people who had developed the plans for Disney World, back when Orlando was little more than a humid, central Florida city. Following that project, Quinn was planning to go out on his own as a consultant with no plans to work for anyone else.

We started talking, and he said he would do some consulting for the World's Fair, but that he didn't want a full-time job. I persisted and finally got him to come on board for a couple of years. We paid him more as Senior VP in charge of marketing, development, and PR than I made as president and CEO. He was well worth it. We were assembling a top-notch international destination, like Disney, and we needed his input.

Quinn brought top talent with him, as well as some former Disney colleagues. Jim Benedick, for example, set up our entire merchandising program and all the concessions, and signed on all the food and beverage vendors. He negotiated the merchandise sales and ensured the quality, in and of itself a multi-million-dollar challenge. Ed Litrenta was our personnel director, who later became a marketing executive at SeaWorld. Bill Bieberbach was our operations guy and Quinn brought in Bill Francisco later to succeed himself. They were all "Sandy's team," as we called them, and they brought both a professional and unique flavor to the Fair.

One of the essential ingredients that Quinn brought to the Fair was in the presentation. For example, at Disney World, you may have noticed that when people sweep up trash, it makes a noticeable sound. They wanted visitors to notice how they were keeping the park clean. Everything was "part of the show." Even if the job was as simple as cleaning up, that staff person was still a vital part of the overall show experience. That's the approach we needed and that's what Quinn and the guys brought to the table.

Plus, these jobs were temporary. By treaty, we were going out of business on October 31, 1982. We didn't have time to bring people in and develop the talent. We just brought in mostly young people, who gained experience on the job with public relations and marketing and all the operational people. They were qualified because Quinn said they were qualified, and he showed them the ropes. And, they were successful.

So, I give myself credit for recruiting Quinn, like any good college football coach would do when scouting an ace quarterback. And, I give Quinn and the guys credit for their major contributions to our World's Fair, and should point out that many of them went on to consult at other World's Fairs around the world, or with major attractions the world over.

Bo's Lifelines: Cookie, Jack, Jon, and Rick

As the Fair quickly approached, I assembled a small staff of secondary personnel to assist me in my daily duties, my "lifelines." Cookie Crowson did for me what I had done for the governor: she decided who I should or shouldn't talk to. As my executive assistant, she kept my schedule, handled my appointments, and generally steered me in the right direction. She was a delightful people person, as well.

When I met with our subcommittee on compensation one year, I recommended Crowson for a significant jump in salary. She truly was my lifeline and was as important to me and management as any of my top four or five people. So, she got a tremendous pay raise, despite some on that subcommittee—and it was nearly all men—who were taken aback. Judging by their reactions, you would have thought her raise alone would disrupt the Knoxville economy. They all had their own "Cookies," and they knew they weren't paying them nearly enough. But, she was worth fighting for; her role was that important. Gender parity today is far from perfect, but I think it's vastly improved from the days when the phrase didn't exist.

Another part of my lifeline was Jack Rankin. Early on, he wanted to be involved in the Fair effort, but we didn't have the money to hire him. So, in an admittedly somewhat questionable move, I convinced the mayor to hire him as a city employee and loan him to us at the Fair.

Rankin was a singularly determined man. If you didn't want something done, you didn't ask Rankin. If you wanted a wall torn down, you'd better have been sure, because Rankin would have torn it down on the word "go." He wasn't exactly a diplomat—but he was quite a doer.

One of Rankin's job duties ended up being improvised. At a reception within a year of the Fair's grand opening, I had a few glasses of wine. I lived only a few miles from the Fair site and drove myself home. I got a call on my car phone, a mobile radio device at a time when that equipment took up half the trunk. Pulling over on the side of the highway so I could take the call, I soon saw police blue lights behind me. I said I'd call my caller back.

I was fairly well-known in the area from press conferences and media appearances, so the patrolman recognized me as I rolled my window down. He asked if I'd had anything to drink. I answered "a couple of glasses of wine." He said, "Frankly, Mr. Roberts, you smell like a winery." He said he had seen me parked slightly askew and appearing slumped over as I talked on the phone.

The young patrolman stood there, weighing his options. It would have been press worthy if I had been arrested, and I certainly deserved it. I remember thinking that my career and my future lay in the hands of this 25-year-old policeman.

He finally asked how far away I lived. He followed me home, and I arrived safely. I decided at that point that I needed a driver—not that I was a heavy drinker by any stretch of the imagination, but I enjoyed a glass of wine. No more taking any chances. Rankin became my driver for the duration of the Fair.

Rounding out Cookie's crew of lifelines were Jon Brock and Rick Jacobs. Both were brilliant 23-year-olds. Brock came from a prominent family in a small Kentucky town. Recently graduated from UT, he was working as a junior lobbyist for the Tennessee Coal Association and had the confidence necessary to leave his job to temporarily work at the Fair. Jacobs, who had grown up in Oak Ridge where his father was a scientist, was fresh out of Georgetown University with a major in Russian studies.

Brock and Jacobs first prepared me for all of my trips abroad, including schedule, logistics, information about every person I was meeting and every country to which I would be traveling. Their standard of excellence spoiled me and I became more and more dependent on their advance work and unbelievable ability to anticipate what I might need. Then, virtually every day at the Fair there were either one or more ceremonies, which they would plan, write the remarks for me, coordinate with other staff or officials, and hand me a booklet as I walked out the door, supremely confident that every detail imaginable had been considered, reviewed and addressed.

Many of the events were similar—welcoming this country, complimenting that exhibit—but some of them stretched beyond a day and involved legions of security. I could look at my prepared notes, whether in advance or as I approached the podium, and know that what Brock and Jacobs had scripted would be beyond perfect. Like that policeman, but under far better circumstances, my professional life and the reputation of the Fair was in the hands of these exceptional 23-year-olds. In fact, I don't know that I've encountered anything like these two since then. Everyone should have been so lucky to have a Brock and a Jacobs.

There were many instances when the World's Fair was also in the hands of this pair. For example, following China's commitment to participate in the Fair, one of the things they requested was a trip to other World's Fair sites in the U.S. Without hesitation, the staff person I assigned to escort them for two weeks during their excursion was Jon Brock. Away the delegation went with Brock as guide, advance man, counselor, confessor, and vital communications link with us in Knoxville. Once during the trip there was an important document which needed to be exchanged by Telex, a fairly new technology in most communities at that time. The delegation was in Seattle, but Brock expertly solved the dilemma by locating a machine at the Seattle Police Department. I remember thinking later, that maybe a Gatlinburg newspaper publisher betting on a 23-year-old editor wasn't taking such a huge risk after all.

That was my team: Cookie, Jack, Jon, and Rick. They had the energy, the knowledge, the reliability, and the loyalty that allowed me to function effectively while running the Fair. My office also included great contributions from Project Control Director Bill Newton and administrative assistant Sharon Wells, whose contributions were invaluable.

When someone once asked me to pinpoint my most important management tool, I laughed and said: "Ignorance." What I honestly meant was that we really didn't know what we *couldn't* do; if we had listened (and I'm talking about myself, as well as all of the supporters and leaders from Knoxville and beyond) to the chorus of critics and the scads of skeptics, we would have accomplished nothing. We didn't have time to allow negativity to define us. If I had to narrow my contribution to a single word it would be *prioritizing*. I had to constantly shuffle time and efforts to manage the question of what do we have to do today to still be alive tomorrow? I think the basic journalistic training to write a lead, summarizing in one sentence the essence of a story and why one should continue reading, was an asset.

Opening Day

Saturday, May 1, 1982 was a dazzling, gorgeous day, 75 degrees and sunny. There would be no rain on our parade on Opening Day.

I was often asked, "Are you going to open on time?"

I always responded, "That's the wrong question. We're going to open May 1st because, by international treaty, this World's Fair opens on May 1, 1982. The question is are *we* going to be ready?" For that answer, I'd often look to Ed Keen, our VP of construction, a 6'8" giant of a man, for reassurance. I had complete confidence in him.

The answer was *yes*, we were ready.

After years of hard work, on what had been 70-plus acres of dilapidated buildings and abandoned rail yards, now stood 225,000-square-feet of colorful exposition space occupied by 22 countries, six states, and 90 corporations. Anchored by the gleaming green and gold Sunsphere tower, the "Waters of the World" manmade lake, and the Court of Flags, we welcomed more than 87,000 visitors on that first day. A local newspaper headline proudly proclaimed, "It's Real, Folks! World's Fair Opens Gates Wide"——perhaps in a rebuke to *The Wall Street Journal*'s now-famous, condescendingly reported story of 1980. Another media outlet reported that guests were lining up as early as 3 a.m. waiting for the gates to swing wide on Opening Day.

President Ronald Reagan attended and delivered the keynote speech at the opening ceremony, with Tennessee native Dinah Shore serving as mistress of ceremonies. This World's Fair had straddled three presidencies, from Ford to Carter to Reagan. They'd all been supportive, especially the Carter and Reagan administrations, and Opening Day was a refreshingly nonpartisan affair. With the entire opening proceeding nationally televised, the 1982 World's Fair was finally receiving attention and credibility relative to the extraordinary amount of work put into its origination by the community, the state, the U.S. government and the thousands of others who worked to bring it to fruition.

We did single out Stewart Evans for special recognition on that day, but how could we have possibly ever done his justice to his conceiving the idea for Knoxville? Bryant Gumbel, who was one of the world's premier broadcasters at the time, spent a week at the Fair with *The Today Show* airing live every morning at 7 a.m.

One of the most important things about Opening Day for me is what *didn't* happen. The original plan was to have paratroopers parachute in with an American flag which would be raised on a flagpole during the national anthem. Looking at the somewhat constricted space, I felt that the idea had too many possibilities for problems with far too many things that could go wrong. It wasn't that I was risk-averse—I wouldn't have been involved in the World's Fair if that had been the case. But I didn't want the excitement of Opening Day with the nation and the world watching, to be hijacked by a potential disaster. I nixed the idea, one of the few times I completely vetoed something. It wouldn't be the last I'd hear of this decision, though.

A little-known ceremony that happened away from the site on Opening Day, was the fulfillment of a promise. Early in our formative days, we were hosting an event at the Hyatt Regency Hotel (Knoxville's finest at that time), while one of the national chain's owners (a member of the wealthy, influential Pritzker family from Chicago) was in town for a visit. He asked Paul Sherbakoff, general manager and veteran hotelier in Knoxville, who was also a steadfast supporter of our efforts, about the purpose of the event. Sherbakoff explained what was going on, and the amazed guest replied in a tone of disbelief: "If you guys pull this off, I'll kiss your a..s right here in the middle of the lobby." And, so, at 3:30 p.m. on our historic Opening Day, Sherbakoff had a mule escorted into the Hyatt's luxurious lobby where the Pritzker family member dutifully kept his promise. Yes, he did kiss the back end of the beast. I broke away from the Fair site to take part in that ceremony...it was an especially fitting tribute to Knoxville's ambition realized.

Following Opening Day, we got up to do it again 183 more times. I was hell-bent on living for every moment. And, I did.

The World, Day-to-Day

As Ethrage J. Parker, Tennessee's Commissioner of Tourist Development said, "A World's Fair is Opryland, Disneyland, the Smithsonian, the United Nations, a state fair, a country fair, and a marching band, all rolled into one."

Every hour, every minute of the day, from 10 a.m. to 10 p.m., there was something fun and informative happening at the World's Fair. We had the international exhibits, from Peru to the Philippines and

Saudi Arabia to South Korea, and the corporate exhibits, from Ford Motor Company to General Electric to Texaco, among others. We had parades and roving comedians, mimes, and costume characters. There were outdoor performances in the Tennessee Amphitheatre, plus children's events. We used the Disney approach, tastefully adapted by Sandy Quinn, of keeping people entertained while they waited in line (there was always a line somewhere on site), particularly for the exceedingly popular Chinese exhibit. More than 90 places offered food and drink, from the chili and Fritos served in a bag (aka "Petros," the popular snack concoction introduced by Joe and Carole Schoentrup of Spokane with assistance from East Tennesseans Dale, Randy and Keith Widmer) to the German Strohaus fare to Belgian waffles, to the local favorite, Buddy's bar-b-q. (An early sponsor of the Fair, Buddy's was so popular that he rewarded his on-site staff with a vacation to Hawaii after the Fair's close.)

We closed every night with an unforgettable fireworks show. There were two Italian families, the Zambellis and the Gruccis, who were the biggest names in pyrotechnics at that time. We split the contract between the two, so that one family produced the first 90 days of the Fair and the other did the final 90 days. I learned a lot about fireworks during that experience—namely, that they are absurdly expensive. We spent $35,000 every single night, which would be equivalent to spending $100,000 in 2022 dollars. Still, we considered it a bargain. It was a full, sensory overload experience every evening. Many people in the community, whether on-site or not, gathered by 10:30 p.m., rain or shine, to hear the explosions as they watched the skies light up with magnificent colors. These expertly choreographed shows represented the most cutting-edge pyrotechnics of the time and provided a spectacular finale to every day. They were also one of my favorite things about the Fair.

On the Fourth of July, we, along with the U.S. Pavilion, presented the "Star Spangled Spectacular," a special celebration at Neyland Stadium featuring a sensational, hour-long fireworks and laser show—which some pyrotechnics aficionados described as the largest fireworks event in history. I don't recall precisely which of the two Italian families produced it—they may have even joined forces for such a massive display. To kick-off the sold-out show, a plane flew over the middle of the football field. A trooper parachuted in bearing the U.S. and Tennessee flags to present to me. I thanked him for doing the show. He said, "Well, thank you for letting us do it *this time*, Mr. Roberts." From the tone in his voice, I sensed that they still begrudged the fact that I had nixed the World's Fair Opening Day parachute presentation, but I shrugged it off. After all, there were almost 50,000 people waiting for us to bring Johnny Cash and June Carter Cash onstage.

My office was on the top floor of the former L&N Station. I'd usually walk through the site after morning meetings. I could look out my window at the waiting line to the Chinese pavilion shortly after our 10 a.m. opening and estimate the day's attendance within 5,000 people. We averaged 60,000 visitors a day. Sometimes, I could tell we'd have 80,000 or more. On October 9th, we broke 100,000 (102,842), which was also the day when we celebrated former President Jimmy Carter. Those record-breaking attendance days stretched our staff close to the breaking point, but we made it through.

* * *

The Fair always had an operational "officer of the day." That was a senior person (Ed Keen, Charlie Smith, George Siler, et al) who had the authority to make immediate executive decisions about pressing problems. The third day of the World's Fair fell on a Monday. We had huge crowds on Saturday (Opening Day) and on Sunday, but our projections for that Monday were around 35,000, more than a 50% drop projected from Saturday. We staffed our front gates accordingly.

Massive lines, eventually reaching 57,000 people, were backing up for the 10 a.m. opening. Ed Keen, as the operations officer of the day, called me and said we had a major catastrophe on our hands. He recommended just opening the gates and admitting everyone, en masse, in as orderly a fashion as possible. I gave the green light to that advice. Most of the visitors already had their tickets in hand, and the potential revenue loss incurred would be nothing compared to the disastrous public relations that would have ensued if we had left throngs of restless attendees waiting under the broiling sun. It was a very good call on Keen's part.

* * *

During the Fair, there were ceremonies of some kind every day. Each country had its own national day, if not days, with its own unique style and entertainment. One of the early celebrations was Great Britain Day, which was accompanied, that evening, by an off-site performance by the musician-owned London Symphony Orchestra. I arrived early, so I stepped outside of the auditorium to indulge in my only acknowledged sin: smoking a pipe. As I puffed away, I saw something in Knoxville, Tennessee that I never imagined I would ever see there. Scalpers were selling tickets to attend the performance. I was accustomed to seeing that at a football or a basketball game, but I never envisioned that I would see people haggling over symphony tickets. Those who attended enjoyed a never-to-be repeated concert, as the musicians presented a strikingly beautiful program. Yep, our "scruffy little city" proudly reared its head yet once again.

* * *

For the Philippines National Day, First Lady Madame Imelda Marcos arrived to represent her country. I first met her in New York City in a meeting at the Waldorf Towers in 1980. As I was welcomed into her suite, I was taken aback by the number of flower arrangements (they were massively astonishing, beyond colossal; I've never seen anything like them either before or since) adorning the space. When she entered the room, she owned it. She's a dominant personality, who was charismatic and very charming. She agreed that the Philippines would participate in the Fair.

Later, as I saw the Philippines exhibit beginning to take shape as it was under construction, I took a chance and contacted her. Knowing her high aesthetic standards, I reluctantly informed her that I was concerned that she might not be satisfied with the quality of her nation's presentation. She took care of the issue, pronto. The exhibit was quickly upgraded with an accompanying increase in the budget. When she arrived before her country's national day, I greeted her at the airport. As we rode to the Fair site in a chauffeured car, I said, "Madame Marcos, I think you're going to be quite proud of your exhibit." Her response: "Mr. Roberts, I think the more important thing is, do *you* like it?" Her point was taken. I appreciated that she let me know my opinion mattered to her, but at a cost.

After two gruesome days of successful official ceremonies, receptions and parties, I again found myself with her in a limousine following the party that she personally hosted at the Hyatt Regency Hotel. We were taking her and her entourage, the "Blue Ladies" (a coterie of older women with graying hair tinted blue), to her waiting private 747 at the airport. It had been another enjoyable, but brutally long day. It was 1:30 a.m. and I wanted to loosen my tie and have a relaxing, informal exchange with her. We'd been through a lot together. But, instead, she proceeded to outline her plans for a pre-K student program she was planning to introduce in the Philippines. She was all business, all the time. An interesting, formidable woman, despite the legal and political troubles which would later befall her and her husband. (Oh, and, in case readers are wondering, yes, she did wear fabulous shoes, according to those with knowledge of bespoke footwear. She was pilloried in the press for the 1,060 pairs of shoes in her collection.)

* * *

The Chinese Ambassador to the U.S. was the ranking visitor and host for the People's Republic of China's national day events. During my visits to China, I recalled my hosts serving me Kweichow Moutai, which I'd best describe as Chinese moonshine. As I sipped the lethal stuff (it's distilled from fermented sorghum) after toasts, they watched me closely, but I held my own. Now, back in Tennessee, with them as my guests, I had the pleasure of reciprocating the hospitality I had received in their country.

I dispatched a staff member (Jack Rankin, of course) to the infamous town of Newport, not far from the East Tennessee mountains to see about procuring some moonshine. We hosted the ambassador in Gatlinburg for our official "state dinner" and served delicious Tennessee country food: country ham, potatoes, beans, collard greens, biscuits with gravy and other Southern delicacies. And, yes, we proudly served Tennessee "White Lightning" moonshine. We toasted dozens of times as the Chinese ambassador sturdily held his own. Like the rest of us, though, he was getting well-lubricated.

Our transportation back to Knoxville was provided by Litton Cochran's luxurious McDonald's bus which he graciously loaned us to ferry dignitaries whenever needed. As we passed through the Mountain View Hotel (a true reflection of an Appalachian Mountains experience) lobby on our way out, there was an entertainer playing his guitar for guests. The ambassador impulsively asked for the guitar and took it with him on the bus. He started playing, sort of, and improvised a song about being in the mountains and "drinking that special Tennessee wine." He was quite a contrast in comparison with Madame Marcos. We had a terrific time on that ride back to Knoxville, and I eventually ensured that the purloined instrument was returned, with compensation, to its rightful owner.

A Rousing Royal Celebration

The United Kingdom's (UK) National Week celebration at the Fair became historic, when on June 21, 1982, Diana, Princess of Wales gave birth to her first child with Charles, the Prince of Wales. The second in line to the throne, Prince William, Duke of Cambridge, was born at

9:03 p.m. in London, which would've been about 4 o'clock Knoxville time the next day. The staff at the UK Pavilion was ecstatic. They hung a large sign out front proclaiming: "It's A Boy!" They then proceeded to close their pavilion early, invited our staff and fellow international pavilion staff members to join them, turning their exhibit into one of the most jubilant, makeshift British pubs to ever exist in the U.S. They declared, "let the succession and the party begin" and boy, did it.

Afterward, I was asked if we had planned the UK celebrations around Princess Diana's projected delivery date as a showcase marketing moment? I laughed and said I would love to say that was the case, but that I was fairly certain that the dates for their week-long festivities had been scheduled to accommodate their ambassador's availability to travel to Knoxville. It was a completely serendipitous occurrence.

Mixing Cultures, Japan Shines

The Japanese brought the internationally famous Kabuki Theatre ensemble to Knoxville, where men play both male and female roles in colorful costumes, their faces painted with oshiroi, a thick white makeup derived from rice powder. Prior to the Fair, the Japanese ambassador had invited me to join him in New York City to announce the Kabuki's planned appearance at the Fair. This coincided with the forthcoming release of the movie *Tootsie,* scheduled for the end of the year, in which Dustin Hoffman played an actor masquerading as a woman.

Hoffman joined us for the announcement and had the Japanese completely enthralled. They were fascinated by this diminutive American icon, who had acted in a movie role that paralleled their own Kabuki performances. They were completely swept away by his appearance that day, and by the fact that at 5'6" he was the same height as the average Japanese man. The World's Fair audiences were fascinated by the Kabuki presentations as well, as it gave a chance to share in the ancient art.

Stars Galore Sparkled at the World's Fair

In addition to the international days, scores of world-class performers appeared at the Fair. Ballet dancer Rudolph Nureyev performed. Bob Hope celebrated his 79th birthday with us. Australia sent Air Supply to play their then-chart-topping soft rock hits during its national days. This being Tennessee, there was a steady stream of the country's biggest names of the day, from Kenny Rogers to Loretta Lynn to Jerry Lee Lewis to Dolly Parton to Glen Campbell to Johnny Cash and Willie Nelson. It was 184 days of all-star entertainment.

One of the most moving moments was the Warsaw Philharmonic Orchestra's performance of Rachmaninoff's *Symphony No.2* in the Tennessee Amphitheatre. Every single seat (of the 1443 available) was filled. It was a particularly poignant time in Poland's history as the country was still under Soviet rule, but a burgeoning Solidarity movement was catching the imagination and courage of its people. At some point during the performance, several young people hoisted a "Solidarity" banner. The players responded approvingly with taps of their bows. At the conclusion of the program, the crowd stood and clapped wildly in a standing ovation that seemed as though it might never end. I've rarely been more proud to be an American.

We also had a sports program, the first World's Fair to focus attention on that area of human endeavor. Bill Schmidt, an Olympic bronze medalist in the javelin throw, who earned a MS in Business Education from UT, directed our athletic events. Among the highlights: The Pittsburgh Steelers beat the New England Patriots (24-20) in a preseason game before a record crowd of more than 90,000 fans at Neyland Stadium, while the Boston Celtics played the Philadelphia 76ers in UT's Stokely Athletic Center (where Larry Bird actually got into a fight during the *exhibition* game).

There was also international baseball with a visit by Major League Commissioner Bowie Kuhn, boxing, tennis, a motocross world cup, a demonstration by the U.S. Olympic gymnastic team on-site and at the Fourth of July celebration at Neyland Stadium, and other high-profile events throughout the six months. I don't want to take sole credit for including sports, but my lifelong love for the beauty of competition was the primary reason that we "played the games" at the World's Fair.

Some 1982 "Firsts" Introduced in Knoxville

There were several "reveals" or introductions of revolutionary ideas and experiences at the Fair. Highly significant was an invention by Dr. Sam Hurst, the most prolific scientist (with 34 patents to his credit) at nearby Oak Ridge National Laboratory. His idea for "The Resistive Touchscreen Technology," debuted at the Fair in the U.S. Pavilion, and was demonstrated at 33 locations throughout the site. Hurst's somewhat unheralded concept for a transparent screen led directly to the ubiquitous touchscreen technology used around the world today.

The Texaco corporate exhibit introduced a novel idea, which at the time seemed a bit unlikely for widespread, future use: the Pay-at-the-Pump concept, configured to accept credit cards so that users could pump their own gasoline (I'm sure many folks thought, what a crazy idea; that will never happen).

The Goliath of the soft drink beverage industry, the Coca-Cola Company, used the Fair's 11 million visitors to introduce and test new Cola flavors. The winning flavor, hands-down, was Cherry Coke, which was ready for mainstream production and distribution in 1985.

Dairymen, Inc., a milk farmers' cooperative of 8,000 eastern and Southeastern dairymen, introduced its Tetra Pak (UHT), no refrigeration needed, three-month shelf life milk product at the Fair. It was particularly appropriate for the Dairymen to bring that product to the public's attention in Knoxville, as the technology had been developed by UT-K alumnus, Dr. William Roberts. He was showcased with his invention in *People* magazine in the fall of 1982.

Appalachian Folklife and Real Moonshine

The Stokely-Van Camp Folklife Festival, ably directed by Dick Van Kleeck, offered Fair guests a chance to inspect and learn about mountain artifacts, and the cornerstone foods of nutritional Southern sustenance (cornbread, hominy and biscuits), in a curated Appalachian setting. Moonshine maker Hamper McBee, featured in a PBS documentary entitled, *Raw Mash,* demonstrated the fine art of crafting 'shine, using an authentic moonshine. McBee's product was lawfully destroyed each evening at closing time, per the strict conditions of K.I.E.E. 's contractual agreement with Federal officials. The Folklife Festival was an attraction unto itself, an extremely popular spot with out-of-region visitors, who were fascinated to see the mountain life-style and experience its incredible music up close.

Energy Turned the World at Three Symposia

Energy scientists from throughout the world gathered in Knoxville on three occasions to exchange ideas, explore new technological trends and to collaborate on measures for addressing one of the planet's most crucial issues: energy use, production, development, and alternatives. Eleven countries sent experts to participate in the first symposium, held in Oct. of 1980, the second in Nov. of 1981, and for the finale meeting, held three weeks after the Fair opened in May 1982.

The symposia were organized and conducted by my man for all seasons, Walter Lambert. Reports were circulated to all participating nations, as well as to appropriate U.N. committees and agencies. Though no major "wow" solutions were produced (nor expected), one of the most significant results, cited by everyone involved, was bringing the "field of energy" as a topic to international attention. (As mentioned earlier, Lambert finished that job, and at my request, proceeded to organize and conduct an independent group of officials and private sector leaders to generate a plan for the redevelopment of the Fair site. The innovative plan they revealed in October 1982 included a funding source, and defined a path to an exciting, mixed-use development.)

Painting the Media Picture

As with almost any mammoth undertaking, the media plays a significant role and becomes a part, especially in our case, of whether or not the event will actually happen and, if so, whether or not it will be a success.

Overall, I believe we had fair coverage. After all, that's what one would hope they would receive. Certainly the coverage was extensive locally during those early years. I always tried to be transparent, and truthful in dealing with the media. Having been trained in the profession, and practicing it (in an admittedly small way), I was highly respectful of the job and all that it entailed.

Not long after the early efforts proved that the event was going to be seriously pursued, an opposition group emerged. Joe Dodd, an associate professor of political science at UT, and Leon Ridenour, became the unofficial spokesmen for a loosely organized citizen's opposition group. This was to be expected, and they played a role in addressing matters that deserved our attention and concern. Frankly, they did an impeccable job of keeping us on our toes. The only time I got frustrated was when, during a forum, they stated that the crowds were going to change and ruin "our" Knoxville. Then, later on, they changed tactics by insisting that if we were successful in having a World's Fair that it would ultimately fail because no one would attend.....at that point I always responded with the same statement: "Make up your minds, gentlemen."

As we moved closer to reality, the media coverage moved from local to statewide, and then to regional and onto the national scene. Though

I felt comfortable dealing with the media, we decided that I should participate in the special training offered by our national public relations firm, Hill & Knowlton in New York. It was an interesting two days. I learned a few things that I didn't already know, but the main takeaway was that the media are important, and rather than having me rush from meeting-to-meeting and then dash into a press conference, I should (and did) set aside blocks of time, to be briefed by my able staff on issues which might arise, and/or to review and discuss what we should present. They also wisely advised that I then take an additional 15 minutes, alone without distractions, to mentally process the information, and to focus prior to dealing with the 20 or 30 people who could carry messages, good and/or bad, to millions of people.

Other than the negative *Wall Street Journal* article that turned out to be a benefit in terms of rallying local support, there were only two other instances where I felt we needed a different approach. The first came as we were negotiating the final documents and terms for the multi-level financing plan. Ernie Beazley, an astute, energetic, headline-seeking reporter for the *Knoxville Journal* had an inside connection with folks from one of the local banks, which was not a Fair supporter.

Additionally, Beazley's father was a banker, who, seemingly, kept him supplied with an arsenal of leading questions. He produced daily, over-amplified reports, "exposing" problems with terms, timelines, and other minutiae that anyone who has been through a detailed financial agreement would view simply "as a matter of course." His reporting was factual but always carried an unjustified, snarky undertone. The daily hammering was making our cadre of naturally conservative lenders and financial people uneasy.

Finally, a committee from the Board of Directors and myself met with the publisher of the *Journal* and put it on the table: we were not going to be able to close the Fair loan if the Beazley stories continued to appear. We said: "If you find anything wrong, or any wrongdoing by anyone, then by all means, expose it immediately."

We added that *if* the type of exaggerated coverage that the issue was receiving in the *Journal* continued, that there would be no loan document and no World's Fair. To his credit, the publisher reassigned his irrepressible reporter, so that we could proceed in closing the loan and in having a Fair.

One other incident transpired not long after the Fair's debut. We made a mistake when we released the forecasts of daily attendance that the original ERA report had detailed to illustrate how a total of 11 million visitors would attend the exposition. The forecast was a bit low for our Opening Day attendance, and a tad high for the next day's (Sunday) attendance. The forecast was for 60,000 visitors while the actual number on Sunday was 40,001.

No big deal, or so we thought. Wrong.

Since all of the reports we were getting in the local media were not from wire services, we were not always immediately aware of what the wire services were disseminating. A few days into the Fair, I began receiving calls from friends in other states, saying how sorry they were that we were having trouble. I couldn't imagine what they were talking about, but asked the staff to look into it. They discovered that one of the wire services, United Press International (UPI) , had released a story on the Monday after Opening Day that the Knoxville

Fair was having problems with huge drops in attendance, based on that Sunday's number. We were stunned, particularly because the Monday forecast of 30,000 was so low, when we had nearly twice that number of attendees.

That UPI reporter continued to feed unfavorable stories out on the wire service. We weren't sure why he was doing this, but we accumulated quite a portfolio of negative UPI reports. Our national public relations firm asked for, and was granted, a meeting with the regional heads of UPI. They met in my office, and viewed our exhaustive presentation, which documented what had been filed compared to what the actual facts were (the stories went well beyond that initial damaging story). To their credit, and frankly, to our surprise, UPI reassigned its reporter. While we couldn't erase the unnecessary, unjustified damage, the stream of over-played, negative reports did come to a halt.

Otherwise, I believe that the coverage was reasonably fair. We particularly liked the live national telecasts and the lighthearted stories that reporters from across the nation and around the world filed from the Fair site on a regular basis. Their stories accurately conveyed the stunning array of entertainment that was programmed on-site every single day, along with the frivolity of the fairgoers. It was a place where people had an unimaginable amount of unrestrained, pure fun.

I did hundreds upon hundreds of interviews before and during the Fair, but two of my Top Ten favorite media memories included: a live interview with Joan Lunden, co-anchor of ABC's *Good Morning America*, in the network's New York studio reviewing the Fair site model with her, and exchanging waves with NBC's Jane Pauley and Bryant Gumbel as I made my way to the office every morning during the first week of operation.

Not too long after the Fair's debut, we were fortunate enough to benefit from the high-level skills of a senior public relations executive, on loan from the Memphis-based Federal Express (now FedEx) Corporation, one of the Fair's major sponsors. Founder and Chairman Fred W. Smith was kind enough to ask his top public relations veteran, C. William (Bill) Carroll, to accept a special assignment in East Tennessee. Carroll, who had served in the Marines, was an affable, able addition to the K.I.E.E. Management Team. His subtle, yet commanding presence, provided the mature hand needed to steer our youthful crew of media professionals.

* * *

Being president of the World's Fair brought its perks, particularly for my mother, Vera, in meeting some of the stars. She was a huge fan of comedian Red Skelton, having seen him perform vaudeville as a teenager growing up in her native Atlanta. While Skelton was in town, I arranged a dinner at our house so that my mother could meet him. He was a very cordial man, and as funny, or funnier, in real life as he was on stage.

My mother also had the privilege of meeting former President Carter. He had been so instrumental in developing the Fair, that we dedicated a special day, October 9, in his honor. (Incidentally, that day had our highest attendance at more than 102,000 visitors, but whether that was due to Carter's presence or not was unknown.) I introduced him to my mother at a reception. While I am a well-known Democrat (who occasionally voted for Republicans, but never let my Mom know about it), the term "yellow dog Democrat" is far too pale a description for my mother. She was beyond thrilled to get to hug a former Democratic president, who was also a fellow Georgian.

* * *

I even got in on the daily Fair entertainment. We had performers and costumed characters throughout the site to entertain people in line. As a good manager, I felt I should personally try doing as many of the different jobs as possible, for the experience, if for nothing else. In a t-shirt and swim trunks, I donned an oversized bear costume and worked my way through the crowds. It was fascinating. People aren't looking at you; they're looking at the character; the reactions of the children were priceless. I (unwisely) performed my experiment on a witheringly hot July afternoon. I lasted all of 30 minutes before I had to return to the changing room to rehydrate and dry off. I also gained an entirely new level of respect for those guys and gals who performed in those costumes, day and night, regardless of the weather.

* * *

Attending an extraordinary number of events and activities could get rote and repetitive for me, but I kept in mind that for the honorees and the guests at every event, it might be their first and only time at this or any other World's Fair. I wanted every presentation to be special and executed with a high level of energy. That's the mindset that I tried to practice and to instill in every member of our staff. It didn't matter if we were doing an event for the 50th time; we had to bring positive energy to it. We couldn't take anything for granted. It didn't matter if we were interacting with a guest or showing a VIP such as Bob Hope around the site. We wanted to make it a unique, and a once-in-a-life-time experience. We worked diligently at doing that every day. As you might imagine, there were 184 indescribably special days.

* * *

On the penultimate day of the Fair, October 30th, we recorded our 11 millionth visitor, hitting our target attendance number. It was a high note moment. Executive Vice President Ed Keen got on the Fair-wide intercom system to make the announcement. He said, "Hey, guys and gals, ladies and gentlemen——today, the 'scruffy little city' did it!"

Fantastic Overview
Best Feature Story About the World's Fair

Sybil Thurman (now Wyatt) wrote an outstanding special report about the World's Fair for *Aramco World*, a publication of the Saudi Aramco oil company. A former reporter for the *Knoxville News-Sentinel* and a UTK Journalism School graduate, Thurman captured the magic of the Fair in exceptional detail. In fact, her feature story mentioned several things that were actually news to me. Rather than attempt to re-high-light the Fair myself, I asked if I might share her take on "our Fair." I thought her reporting offered as faithful and well-written view of what the event *was* as anything published that year. In fact, it remind-ed me that yes, *you had to be there.*

"The World's Fair: 1982 – A Special Report"
Written by Sybil Thurman

They're used to it now – the crowds, the bands, the laser beams raking the sky at night, the brilliant bloom of fireworks – but back in May, Knoxville's people were openly and unabashedly excited as the guns went off, the balloons went up and a presidential cavalcade swept up the Court of Flags to open the 1982 World's Fair.

To an extent, this sense of excitement still permeates the city. Despite early fears of failure, and fierce opposition, most of Knoxville has come to agree with what Joe Rodgers, commissioner of the U.S. pavilion, said about the fair, "The focus is on the fun."

To the promoters and backers of the fair, of course, the pressure and problems of the fair were hardly fun. They, after all, were responsible for what the *Economist* later described as Knoxville's "cheeky" gamble: the $800-million effort to hold a genuine world's fair in a small, relatively unknown southern city. And during the first weekend, when opening day crowds seemed to sag a little, cab drivers and the owners of motels and inns were heard to inquire – with just a faint note of concern – "What did all think of our fair?" Most of Knoxville, however, just took it as it came, doing what they could and shrugging if they couldn't. The night before the opening, for example, as construction crews raced to complete unfinished exhibits and pavilions, clusters of visitors and what seemed to be most of Knoxville's population gathered on the green slopes of the University of Tennessee above the fairgrounds or strolled casually along Broadway – where a great billboard, had, for 1,000 days, ticked off the days remaining until the fair opened. Others dined leisurely in such places as the balcony of the old L & N (for Louisville and Nashville) railroad station, a huge, 19th-century monument of red bricks and granite slabs converted, by imaginative architects, into a warren of shops and restaurants for the fair.

From such perches, and from bridges that cross the ravine where the fairgrounds lie, these early crowds patiently watched and waited. They were amiable. They were casual. They were relaxed.

Since then, this easy-going attitude has become an outstanding feature of the fair. On opening day, for example, when tight security for President Reagan kept thousands waiting outside the fairgrounds in the sun, most simply shrugged and waited while the bands played, the majorettes marched, the choirs sang and – a spectacular finale – thousands of multi-colored balloons went soaring into the sky – a symbol the fair, after seven years work to get it off the ground, was aloft at last.

It had, nevertheless, been a race against time. From the moment the Bureau of International Expositions okayed Knoxville, fair officials were never really sure they could do it. Even while Dinah Shore sang and President Reagan spoke, a woman in heels was still vacuuming the rug at North Carolina's exhibit, while a carpenter noisily piled strips of aluminum paneling into a cart.

Some exhibits had worse trouble than that. Panama, for some reason, simply didn't open its pavilion at all. A rare Rembrandt scheduled to headline an art exhibit was delayed five weeks because of insurance troubles. And, across the fairgrounds, the Peruvian pavilion faced a crisis: a leak in the ceiling that occurred when waiters in the 140-seat Peking-style restaurant above the exhibit spilled a 20-gallon vat of wonton soup.

The next day there were still more problems. Ticket sellers at the gates ran out of change and thousands of visitors piled up at the gates in the sun getting angrier by the moment – until quick-thinking fair officials decided to let them in free.

In the small, but well-appointed press center in a brand-new hotel adjacent to the fairgrounds, some of the more than 1,500 reporters who poured into Knoxville for the opening were also given a run-down on the kind of troubles the Fair could expect during the long summer ahead: police spotted and rousted six pickpockets; emergency squads treated a man with a heart condition and firemen extinguished three small fires.

Later, as the nation's schools let out and the tourist tide began to break over the Great Smoky Mountains National Park, the problems worsened. But though the traffic did get a bit heavy and the prices just a mite too high, the people of Knoxville continued to delight in the fact that their small, green city had actually gotten itself a real world's fair.

It is true that fair officials and world press coverage have stressed the playful aspects of the fair – and they should. Each day offered a wondrous variety of sparkling entertainment: marching bands; strolling magicians; mimes and jugglers. Big hits include Appalachian folk dancing, the arts of basket-making, woodcarving, quilting and blacksmithing. Above the south end, America's largest Ferris wheel swoops visitors 148 feet above the ground and each day the famous Anheuser-Busch Clydesdale horses, known for their elegant carriage and fleecy white "stockings," lead parades through the fairgrounds. Finally, every evening, the festivities culminate with spectacular fireworks, and a laser show billed as "the largest laser sky show in history" – swirling colors and sheets of lights visible for miles.

But the pavilions – sponsored by 23 countries and 91 corporations – do not neglect the fair's serious theme either. And though the topic – "Energy Turns the World" – may seem dry, scientists, graphic designers and technicians from around the globe have, with imagination and taste, humanized the most sophisticated technology.

The U.S. pavilion, for example, offers a debate on energy that includes Jane Fonda; China provides river rides in a 20-foot, solar-powered dragon boat; the Tennessee Valley Authority allows visitors to try to match energy demands with available supply in a simulated load-control center; and France shows the core of its nuclear breeder reactor. There is also a look at oil shale, a glimpse of the bottom of the North Sea – via a British oil drilling rig – and an uncomfortably realistic coal mine from West Virginia.

The fair also provides a forum for every exhibitor to show off its state-of-the-art technology. Talking robots discuss energy topics in Japan's pavilion, France presents an electrified model of the Bullet Train – the world's fastest – and Australian windmills up to 75 feet tall pump water to irrigate eucalyptus trees and ferns inside the pavilion.

One of the more memorable attractions is the IMAX theater – with a screen 67 feet high and 90 feet wide – in which the U.S.A. offers an enormous, three-dimensional film on the story of America's energy – past, present and future. Elsewhere in the six-level cantilevered pavilion, visitors can push buttons on 33 "talk-back" computers to get answers to their energy-related questions, and stroll among 12-foot murals and artifacts from six previous fairs and museums in the United States.

Some exhibits mix energy with culture. Korea, for example, demonstrates an ancient floor-heating system called "Ondol" – along with folk dance performances, Tae Kwon Do karate exhibitions and a restaurant serving traditional Korean cuisine.

Germany showcases an 18th-century waterwheel; the Italians pay tribute to the 40th anniversary of the first self-sustaining nuclear chain reaction; and the Canadians operate a 22-foot working model of the world's largest wind turbine.

Although the Hungarian Pavilion addresses world energy problems too, it will be remembered primarily for its Rubik's cube, a giant version of the puzzle invented by Hungarian architect Erno Rubik. The huge cube, which solves itself mechanically every few seconds, is the focal point of Hungary's presentation, but a restaurant serving Hungarian goulash, cabbage rolls, and strudel may be equally memorable.

History, art and culture are also stressed at the fair, particularly at one large pavilion housing China, Egypt, and Peru. The Chinese, who see the fair as an opportunity to establish a cultural dialogue with the world, offer a portion of the Great Wall of China, along with scores of soapstone and jade carvings, modern and antique porcelain, rattan and silk goods, furniture, and tapestries woven with pearls. The pavilion does not neglect energy entirely, however; in addition to the solar boat, it offers a display on the collection of marsh gas for conversion into propane gas. The fair's biggest hit, China's pavilion has crowds waiting up to three hours.

Egypt's exhibit also focuses on history – with a collection of treasures from the Pharaonic, Coptic and Islamic periods. Similarly, Peru celebrates its past with gold and silver relics and a 3,000-year-old mummy.

Some of the exhibits are quite candidly sales promotions – but enjoyable anyway. Many U.S. states make pitches for their tourist attractions with "visual vacations" to Tennessee's Grand Ole Opry, North Carolina's Kitty Hawk, South Carolina's Myrtle Beach, the Kentucky Horse Park, and the Mississippi and North Florida Gulf Coast.

Several states, though, go a step past strict promotion. West Virginia is one, with an exhibit on coal mining that has received international recognition for its accuracy and fairness, and Tennessee, taking its role as host to the world fair seriously, built a $4 million open-air amphitheater in the center of the fair, where an extravagant music and dance production called "Sing Tennessee" is performed; the amphitheater is a futuristic fiberglass tent, one of the few permanent structures on the site.

Outside the fair, Knoxville is offering still more entertainment. At the Knoxville Civic Auditorium and Civic Coliseum, for example, seats are already booked for October with such drawing cards as Rudolf Nureyev, dancing with the Boston Ballet the Royal Tahitian Dance Co., Carlos Montoya, the Scottish National Orchestra, the Prague Symphony, Al Hirt and Pete Fountain, the Dance Theater of Harlem, and the Grand Kabuki of Japan.

In a spirited effort to offer something for everyone, the fair also scheduled 19 sporting events, including a round-robin baseball tournament with teams from the U.S., Korea, Japan, and Australia, and a round-robin basketball tourney with teams from the U.S., China, Canada, and Yugoslavia. Among other events are a National Football League exhibition game between the Pittsburgh Steelers and the New England Patriots, a National Basketball Association exhibition game, and PGA Cup matches pitting nine U.S. golf pros against nine pros from Britain and Ireland.

The list goes on, with rowing, canoeing, kayaking, boxing, cycling, gymnastics, hockey, racquetball, rugby, soccer, softball, swimming, tennis, volleyball, weightlifting, wrestling, and road racing. And if that weren't enough, four University of Tennessee home football games will be played during the fair in UT's 91,249-seat Neyland Stadium.

Then there's food. For people who have dreamed of eating and drinking their way around the world, the fair is the answer to a prayer. Fair officials call the site "the largest restaurant in the world," with 81 eating locations. Fourteen restaurants, other than four operated by Mexico, China, Hungary, and Korea, offer homemade pasta, fresh fish (flown in daily), and such Bavarian fare as sauerbraten and wiener schnitzel. Visitors on the move can choose from an enticing assortment of snacks, including stuffed potato skins, fried catfish, baklava, Filipino egg rolls, bagels and lox, New Orleans jambalaya, French pastries, Belgian waffles, country ham and biscuits, and muffins of every description. Fair management predicts that more conventional appetites will tackle some 500 tons of hamburgers, 250 tons of hot dogs, and a million ice cream bars.

From the start, the mood in Knoxville was festive. Color is everywhere. Flags, streamers and banners span the spectrum. Aerial gondola chairs are painted in vibrant reds, oranges and yellows, and the façade of the pavilion housing the European Economic Community is alive with a sunburst mosaic. Even a Knoxville Utility Board substation, located on the site long before anyone dreamed of a World's Fair, has dressed up with bright colors for the occasion.

Knoxville, of course, won't know the results of its "cheeky" gamble until the gates close in October. But higher than expected attendance has given the city – and its creditors – hope that they may not only recoup their investments but recoup them early. If so, everyone will have gotten their money's worth – in cold cash, national attention and fun.

* * *

Complete, Not Closed

Closing Day was on Sunday, October 31st. Some people dressed in costumes for Halloween, but the fact that it was Closing Day dominated the mood. We had a final party with all the international folks following the Closing Day ceremony. Everyone was emotional but also celebratory. My last official line at the Fair was, "I'm not going to declare it closed. I declare it complete." Fireworks followed. Of course, we were somewhat sad but also satisfied. We had done what was supposed to be done for more than 180 days, and we were damned proud of that.

Afterward

I stayed on board for another month or two to wrap things up. There was accounting to do, structures to be dismantled, things to be moved off-site. Essentially, there was a lot of unwinding that the Management Committee needed to do, but it went fairly smoothly.

We held a note-burning ceremony at the Fair in October to torch our debts (figuratively) once we paid them off (literally!). The World's Fair basically broke even with a small surplus; we had hoped to have more, but interest ended up being a considerable expense. Despite all that, and despite being nearly $9 million over budget in interest paid, we were able to pay off all the loans, including all the Energy Expo Ambassadors, the individuals who put up the very first dollars for this highly speculative effort. All those initial investments back in 1977 were paid off, every single bank note was paid off. It was a great celebration. There to wield the torch for the note-burning ceremony was our faithful friend and ardent supporter, Senator Howard H. Baker, Jr. surrounded by many other joyous investors and fantastically happy supporters.

I was proud of the can-do progressive attitude that I'd seen blossom in much of my work, from modernization in Appalachia and Gatlinburg to UT's professionalization to bringing the World's Fair to Knoxville. Regardless of whatever happened afterward, we still had a very successful Fair. Obviously, I'm biased in saying so, but by any metric, we did it very well.

I know, because people told me so. For nearly a decade after the Fair, when I was in public or at a restaurant somewhere in the state, a young person would come over and say, "Excuse me, Mr. Roberts? I just want to tell you that you gave me my first job and how much I enjoyed it. It was the most fun work I've ever done."

The World's Fair started with one employee, me, and ended up with more than 10,000 people working on the site. That included exhibitors, food service employees, ride operators, and other ancillary employees, who had important roles; if you worked there, whatever the job was, it counted. There were another 200 or so people employed by the actual organizing corporation, K.I.E.E. And, every one of us was a person with nothing more than a temporary job.

As a seasoned manager in my late 30s/early 40s, it was invigorating to work with so many savvy, energetic, determined young people. Many of them arrived either straight out of college, or it was their very first job. Being adjacent to the UT campus, we naturally hired a lot of Vols; but, we also had a significant representation of young talent from throughout the state, the country, and yes, from around the world.

There were also some who were secure enough to become part of this challenging journey in mid, or near the end of their careers. Folks like George Siler, who had been head of the Knox County Planning Office, family department-store owner, Jack Proffitt, city councilman Theotis Robinson, who led out successful efforts to achieve our goal of 19% minority participation, and outstanding loaned-executives like Fed-Ex's public relations guru Bill Carroll and TVA attorney Pete Claussen, who served as our in-house legal counsel.

Thinking about those young people reminds me of everything worth celebrating about the Fair and the Knoxville community. Those "youngsters" were not afraid to accept a first job out of college with a definitive ending date. They wanted to be a part of something big, monumental and extraordinary. Their combustible energy, fittingly, fueled the Fair's ultimate success. That says a lot about the involvement and the commitment of people, regardless of their ages.

Thank Goodness for Unnecessary Things

Once, just before the Fair opened, an NBC reporter asked me if I thought that World's Fairs were necessary? I answered, "Absolutely not. They're not necessary for anyone's existence. But, neither are symphonies or ballets or football games or movies or artwork or books. It's the unnecessary things in life that make our journey richer, more fulfilling, and rewarding. So, I say, thank goodness for unnecessary things."

EPILOGUE

I chose to end this book on a high note, as the last chapter wrapped up my final experience as the "youngest" at something.

Some may quibble that I didn't follow through by relating the Butcher Bank failures and how that reflected on the World's Fair image and history. I chose not to do that because there have been thousands of words written about those issues, which transpired with raids and investigations immediately after the Fair came to a close. It was unbelievably sad. Many of the families directly affected were friends and ardent supporters of, not only the World's Fair, but of me, personally. I think it is important to remember that all of the World's Fair debt held by the Butcher family of banks was repaid in full, as were all of the other Knoxville banks and those throughout the country. That was a highlight and a milestone which we celebrated publicly with great fanfare. It's also important to point out that the banks didn't fail *because* of the World's Fair, though, it would not have been possible to succeed without Butcher's personal commitments and the support of his banks.

It was also unfortunate that when Kyle Testerman was re-elected as Knoxville's mayor in 1983 that he didn't capitalize on the Fair's residual potential. I have always characterized him as one of the top people without whose support of the Fair would not have occurred. However, in his second term as mayor, he seemed to devote a lot of energy to settling old political scores, and extracting retribution. This appeared to impact his focus on the Fair site's redevelopment plans, which had been created indepentently of the Fair, and of his immediate predecessor, Mayor Tyree.

A major national corporation, the parent company of developer Fairfield Glade, near Crossville and the Cumberland Mountains, was ready to invest coffers of cash in a mixed-use plan that would have reshaped much of the Fair site and its neighborhood. Finally, it is unfortunate that many in the business community were challenged with a "look what happens when you stick your neck out" syndrome. It wasn't until Bill Haslam became Knoxville's 67th mayor that the city officially recognized and began looking back positively on the World's Fair experience.

I would rather reflect on the thousands of Knoxvillians who expressed their pleasure in hosting an international event in their city, and were delighted to participate in the celebration of it all. Scores of people boasted that they attended almost every single one of the 184 days. I remember seeing the expressions of wonder and merriment on Opening Day, along with the satisfaction and pride at the Closing Day ceremony. Those were among the reasons why, rather than declaring the event closed, I called it "complete."

I remember, like it was yesterday, the look of sheer joy on people's faces. Twice every day, we could guarantee that visitors would be absolutely captivated: when they knew that it was time for the daily parade and when they saw the remarkable Energy Express train (conceived by master showman Bob Jani, another of Sandy Quinn's former Disney talents) coming their way. High school bands from across the nation, led by the professional DuPont World's Fair Marching Band, inspired visitors to clap, cheer and dance spontaneously alongside them. And, when the Energy Express rolled through the site twice daily, blasting its unforgettable theme music, the crowds went absolutely wild. A note about that marvelous music: if you heard it once, you never forgot it. The electronic synth Pop instrumental, composed by Tom Bahler, was completely captivating. A young whiz kid named Don Dorsey arranged, programmed and performed it on an early version of a Synclavier Synthesizer. He was then, and is now, yep, you guessed it—a musical genius with ties to Disney.

Other special memories: The wonderment on children's faces as the larger-than-life costume characters, some on stilts, entertained them; the hordes of happy visitors, fueled by authentic German beer, doing the "Chicken Dance" atop the tables at the always-at-capacity Stroh House; the screams of delight from the riders at Funland, which had one of the tallest Ferris Wheels in the world; the Fair staff overwhelmingly selecting the Australians as the most fun international participants; the waves of applause that swept across the site, hour after hour, every day, in response to the sensational entertainers in the Tennessee Amphitheatre; the gavel banging as it called the members of the Tennessee General Assembly to order in their historic, off-site session held at the Fair; and on, and on, and on.

And, as many guests told me, when they ended their visit with the night's fireworks as the finale, they left satisfied, fulfilled and happily exhausted. They considered it a day well spent.

Before turning to the next "chapters" of my life—working to figure out what I want to be when I finally grow up—two other events that I was primarily responsible for bringing to Knoxville come to mind. First was the 1983 Miss USA pageant, and the other was the 1984 Michael Jackson Victory Tour three-day stand at Neyland Stadium. My next attempt at a book will highlight several stories surrounding those events, which, by the way, were in the *Knoxville Journal's* Top 10 stories of 1983 and 1984. Not surprisingly, those were the *only* positive stories that made the paper's list. As things move on, which they have a tendency to do in life, I'll continue to observe, comment, and occasionally participate in the history of our state and nation, both in life, and in returning to my writing roots with dozens of opinion columns.

Like anyone, were there decisions and actions that I might handle differently if I had the opportunity? Sure. But, then I remember the most famous maxim of my favorite philosopher, Satchel Paige: "Don't look back. Something might be gaining on you." (Originally quoted in *Collier's Magazine,* June 1953.)

* * *

I spent three days combing through the 1982 World's Fair archives at the East Tennessee Historical Society in Knoxville. I wanted to refresh my memory clarify some of my recollection in preparation for writing this book. While I was there I had dinner with my son Sam, his wife, Tammy, and their family at a restaurant on Market Square Mall. It was a Wednesday night. As we walked back to the hotel, we were thrilled to see all the people enjoying themselves in downtown Knoxville, both on the square and on Gay Street. They were telling me how often they came downtown, just to hang out. I thought back to my moment at the Great Wall of China, reflecting on one's life as a "speck in time and space." I thought that, maybe, I might have contributed just a bit to making East Tennessee's historic experience so pleasurable. Even if I hadn't, I was proud of those who had, and I reveled in the moment.

Bo Roberts (center) previewing the World's Fair on ABC's *Good Morning America* in New York with Joan Lunden and David Hartman, left, in 1981.

Commissioner General of the World's Fair (diplomatic appointment by President Ronald Reagan) Dortch Oldham, left, K.I.E.E President Bo Roberts, and Canadian Ambassador to the U.S. Allen E. Gotlieb, right.

Bo Roberts visits with entertainer Kenny Rogers, and his wife, Marianne Gordon Rogers, before the country sensation's performance.

Showing entertainer Bob Hope (left) the Fair from the Sunsphere. *Photo courtesy of Cyndy Waters.*

World's Fair Vice President Theotis Robinson (left) shows a master plan to Paul Bomani of Tanzania, Fatima El Tinay of Sudan and Mohamed Turay of Sierra Leone in 1980.

Bo Roberts on the World's Fair site during construction

The Chinese delegation visited Nashville. At center is host TN Commissioner of Tourist Development Etherage Parker; on the far left is State Museum Curator of Education Lois Riggins-Ezzell, who soon after would be named Executive Director of the Museum. Jon Brock, executive assistant to World's Fair president Bo Roberts, second from right, back row.

TN Senator Howard Baker (left) got a look at the World's Fair model with Bo Roberts at a reception hosted by Secretary of State Alexander Haig in Washington, D.C.

World's Fair Executive Consultant King Cole, left, shares a moment with Bo Roberts in Paris.

Briefing TN Sen. Jim Sasser, right, who would later be appointed Ambassador to China.

With my Mom, Vera, at the Pre-Opening Day Gala. *Photo courtesy of Cyndy Waters.*

Toasting everyone at the Closing Day ceremony, Knoxville First Lady Mary Pat, second from left, and Mayor Randy Tyree, left.

Bo Roberts chats with Secretary General of the Bureau of International Expositions René Chalon, right, following a BIE meeting in Paris.

President Ronald Reagan speaking at the Opening Day ceremonies. Left to right: Jake Butcher, President Reagan, First Lady Nancy Reagan, Bo Roberts.

Sharing a laugh with the former president (right) during the celebration of President Jimmy Carter Day at the World's Fair.

Introducing Tennessee Gov. Lamar Alexander, at left

Philippines First Lady Imelda Marcos with World's Fair Chairman Jake Butcher.
Photo courtesy of Jack Kirkland.

Photo courtesy of Gary Heatherly

中華人民共和國
THE PEOPLE'S REPUBLIC OF CHINA

THE 1982 WORLD'S FAIR

Countdown billboard excitement. *Photo courtesy of Jack Kirkland.*

Photo courtesy of Gary Heatherly

The Goodyear Blimp
was a frequent sight flying
above the World's Fair.
One of the perks of being
President of the Fair was
that I had the opportunity
to do some unique things,
like co-piloting the
Blimp with its pilots.
*Photo courtesy of
Gary Heatherly.*

CAPTAINS OF INDUSTRY!
I called them the best and toughest bosses one could have, the World's Fair Management Committee:
Row 1 Litton Cochran, Chairman Tom Bell, Bo Roberts;
Row 2 Jim Haslam, Jim Bush, Dick Ray;
Row 3 Avon Rollins, I.O. Johnson, Tom Sudman, Bob Pennington;
Row 4 Dick Van Sickle, Dr. Ed Boling;
Row 5 Jack Brennan.

The final International Energy Symposium was held in Knoxville on May 24-27, organized and managed by WF vice president Walter Lambert. *Photo courtesy of Bill Schmidt/1982 World's Fair Collection, Calvin M. McClung Historical Collection, Knox County Public Library, Tennessee.*

WF Executive Vice President for Site Development/Operations Ed Keen (far right) gave a tour to the People's Republic of China delegation. *Photo courtesy of Bill Schmidt/1982 World's Fair Collection, Calvin M. McClung Historical Collection, Knox County Public Library, Tennessee.*

ACKNOWLEDGEMENTS

Wow. Glancing at, and occasionally reading, the Acknowledgements section after completing a book, I've often wondered why some authors list so many people who may have provided them with either personal guidance, heavy lifting in the area of research or fact-checking, emotional support or assistance in any other form. Well, now, I completely understand. The challenge is in not omitting those who were helpful.

It truly took a village (or, maybe, it was several villages?), to assist me in operating at the top of the "Recollection Game," which is actually far more difficult than one might assume. If you ever attempt this, you'll see exactly what I mean. To anyone whom I may have overlooked, I can say that it was not at all intentional. I am grateful for any help that the unsung may have lent.

Now, a huge thanks to:

The Sevier County Village: Historian and author Carroll McMahan provided such a massive amount of assistance that it seems inadequate to simply say thanks, but I do. Carroll sent me to Tim Irvin and the folks at the King Memorial Sevier County Library, who cordially hosted me in their facility for three days, while Sally Hickey happily enlightened me with a trove of salient details about her mother, and Mark Postlewaite did the same about his extraordinary father, the person who pushed me way out front in my very first real job; and, of course, to my sweetheart (since she was six) Cyndy Waters, my host, dinner companion, friend and talented photographer, par excellence—-thank you all.

The Ellington Village: I'll start with the folks at the Tennessee State Library and Archives, who provided a wealth of information that brought back more memories than I could possibly absorb; to Eddie Weeks, the state's Legislative Librarian, who helped straighten me out on several important matters—thank you all so much.

The incomparable Walter Lambert, who qualifies as a one-person, multi-village knowledge guru, who saved my bacon on numerous occasions and in countless ways, but always with a grand sense of incredible humor; and to terrific former colleagues, Claudia Viken and Yvonne Wood, who are still working to keep me straight at every turn—-thanks to this trio of amazing individuals.

The University of Tennessee Village: To the incomparable Joe Johnson, who was a mentor, a role model, and such a deep reservoir of information that he could collectively embarrass the editors of *Encyclopedia Britannica, the World Book Encyclopedia, Funk & Wagnalls New Encyclopedia and the Oxford English Dictionary*; to Lofton Stuart, a marvelously helpful and supportive colleague and friend; to Walter Lambert, yet again, and to Roy Nicks, an icon of public service in higher education and beyond—-thank you, my friends.

The 1982 World's Fair Village: The kind folks at the East Tennessee Historical Society, especially President Warren Dockter, and the Knox County Library McClung Collection for their immense efforts, particularly Joanna Bouldin and Steve Cotham; to the in-depth insights and unforgiving fact-straightener, Jon B. Brock; the encouragement and help of three formidable colleagues *and* friends, Sandy Quinn, Charlie Smith, and Mayor Randy Tyree, for the input and great stories from Cookie Crowson, Pete Claussen, Theotis Robinson, Bill Schmidt, and that Lambert guy, yes, once again; and, to UT-K history professor Shellen Xiao Wu, and her department chair Ernest Freeberg, for producing memories at the China participation celebration, and tremendous last minute help from my friends and great photographers Gary Heatherly, Rip Noel, Mike DuBose, Jack Kirkpatrick along with the aforementioned Cyndy Waters—a grateful thank you to one and all.

The Family Village: To the support and encouragement of my three sons, Sam, Andy and Mark, who all worked in different areas of the World's Fair operation, but were with me in all the other villages, as well; the boys' families were, and are, an inspiration, including their wives, Tammy and Mary, my wonderful grandchildren Drew, Haley, Parker, Haden, Abbey, Annie Jo and Cameron, and their respective spouses, Josh, Bianca, and Tristan, as well as my beloved great-grandchildren, Copeland, Rayne, and Ethan—-a lotta love there for each and every one of these remarkable kids! To the constant support from my brother Gary, his wife Mary Evelyn and my super-niece, Tracy and her family.

The General Village: To the variety of friends who helped me in such a myriad of ways, especially in the computer skills department, where I have often been woefully undertrained; a special thanks to Kevin Rucker, Spencer Bowers, Charlie Clark, Lori Thurston-Smith, and another shout out to my son, Andy, who not only attempted to keep me digitally straight, but provided direction in the overall publishing world, as well. A special shout out to the talented Aldo Amato for saving me from drowning in photos. Though they may not even realize it or connect to it, Howard Gentry, Christie Hauck, Twyman Towery, Keel Hunt, Jim Henry, David and Elizabeth Fox, and Andrew Maraniss, all of whom dutifully listened to my stories, and in spite of that, continued to offer strong encouragement; and, finally, one of my heroes, the late John Seigenthaler, who was firm in his belief that a book was in order following his review of several draft chapters more than a decade ago—-the heartiest of thank you's are in order for each of you.

The Largest Yet Smallest Village: To my enduring icon, the one-woman dynamo, who has supported and encouraged me, her every action and reaction, thoroughly enwrapped and delivered with love, my wife, Leigh Hendry, who just happens to be an exceptionally fine editor, researcher, journalist and writer (in my totally unbiased opinion), this book in any form, but particularly in its final form here—is thanks to her.

If, and that's a big if, there are any grammatical errors or missing commas within these pages, that it is, wholly, completely and undoubtedly, my fault. Thanks Babe.

ADDENDUM I

FOR THE RECORD

THE 1982 WORLD'S FAIR
ORIGIN and DEVELOPMENT

In November 1974, the Downtown Knoxville Association met to consider the recommendation of its Executive Director, W. Stewart Evans, to host an International Exposition in 1980.

This was the origin of what seemed to be an improbable and ambitious plan for the small city of Knoxville, Tennessee to host the world for 184 days.

Some of the highlights of the development:

August 1975
Mayor Kyle Testerman appoints World's Fair Advisory Committee and names Jake Butcher as Chairman and Jim Haslam as Vice Chairman; King Cole selected as consultant

February 1976
The site is selected and incorporated into the city's Lower Second Creek Redevelopment Plan

April 1976
U.S. Department of Commerce turns down 1980 application. S. H. (Bo) Roberts, Jr. elected as President; revised application for 1982 Exposition begun

August 1976
U.S. Department of Commerce approves Knoxville application for 1982 and submits recommendation to Bureau of International Expositions (B.I.E.) in Paris

January 1977
Mayor Randy Tyree recommends and Knoxville City Council approves $11.6 million to procure site

April 1977
President Jimmy Carter requests B.I.E. registration and recommends $20 million for a federal pavilion; the B.I.E. officially sanctions The 1982 World's Fair in Knoxville

October 1978
President Carter announces grants of $12.45 million to the City of Knoxville for the redevelopment project related to The 1982 World's Fair

December 1978
U.S. Secretary of State Cyrus Vance is directed by President Carter to issue invitations to foreign governments to participate in the World's Fair

February 1979
The State of Tennessee approves funds for its pavilion, the Tennessee State Amphitheatre

August 1979
Ceremonies held for 1,000-day countdown

October 1979
Financing arranged for the World's Fair

December 1979
Italy becomes the first foreign nation to participate in the World's Fair

May 1980
Groundbreaking ceremonies are conducted for the construction of the first international pavilion

June 1980
Congress completes appropriation of $20.8 million for participation by the United States

July 1980
France announces its participation; Charles E. Fraser appointed as United States Commissioner General

August 1980
The United Kingdom, the Federal Republic of Germany, and the Commission of European Communities announce their participation

October 1980
The first of three International Energy Symposia is held in Knoxville

January 1981
Japan joins the World's Fair

February 1981
Australia becomes the seventh nation to join

March 1981
Mexico announces participation, followed by the Royal Kingdom of Saudi Arabia

June 1981
Canada and Republic of Korea announce participation

September 1981
Hungarian People's Republic joins the World's Fair

October 1981
The People's Republic of China signs for participation

February 1982
Panama and the Republic of the Philippines announce their plans for participation

March 1982
Arab Republic of Egypt and Peru contract for participation

April 1982
Dortch Oldham named United States Commissioner General

May 1982
President Ronald Reagan officially opens The 1982 World's Fair at 11 a.m. on May 1, 1982

KNOXVILLE INTERNATIONAL ENERGY EXPOSITION

OFFICERS

Jake F. Butcher Chairman,
Board of Directors

James Haslam Vice Chairman,
Board of Directors

S. H. (Bo) Roberts, Jr.
President & Chief Executive Officer

Thomas R. Bell
Chairman, Management Committee, Board of Directors

Roger F. Hibbs
Treasurer

Thomas E Sudman
Secretary

BOARD OF DIRECTORS, THE 1982 WORLD'S FAIR

*Management Committee

** Ex-Officio Member

**Mr. Ben Adams
Chairman
Oak Ridge World's Fair Committee

Mr. Keith Bell
Student, The University of Tennessee
Designated Board Member for UT Student Government Association

*Thomas R. Bell
President
East Tennessee Natural Gas

Mr. David Blumberg
General Agent Emeritus
Massachusetts Mutual Life Insurance Co.

*Dr. Edward J. Boling
President

The University of Tennessee

*Mr. John F. Brennan
Chairman of the Board
H. T. Hackney Company

*Mr. James S. Bush
President
Johnson & Galyon, Inc.

Mr. C. H. Butcher, Jr.
Chairman of the Board
United Southern Bank, Nashville
United American Bank of
Washington County

*Mr. Jake F. Butcher
*Chairman of the Board/Chief
Executive Officer*
United American Bank

Mr. Richard S. Childs
Vice Chairman of the Board
City & County Bank

Mr. William J. Clemons
Real Estate Developer

*Mr. Litton T. Cochran
Owner/Operator
McDonald's Restaurants

Mr. E. B. Copeland
President
E. B. Copeland & Company

Dr. Doris Scott Crawford
Management Consultant

Mr. Ralph D. Culvahouse
Commercial Manager (Retired)
Knoxville Utilities Board

Mr. Roger A. Daley
*President & Business Manager
Knoxville*
News-Sentinel Company

**Mr. Frank H. Deller
Executive Vice President
Greater Knoxville Chamber of
Commerce

*Mrs. Sarah Moore Green
Knoxville City School Board

Ms. Erma G. Greenwood
Attorney
Cramer, Johnson and Greenwood

Mr. Gustav M. Handly
Chairman of the Board (Retired)
Miller's Inc.

Dr. Robert Harvey
Vice President
Knoxville College

*Mr. James Haslam
President
Pilot Oil

*Mr. Roger F. Hibbs
President
Union Carbide – Nuclear Division

Mr. John M. Holliday
President
Knoxville Building &
Construction Trade Council

*Mr. I. O. Johnson
Vice President & General Manager
Robertshaw Controls Company
Fulton Sylphon Division

**The Honorable John R. Johnson
Mayor
City of Morristown

Mr. Eugene L. Joyce
Attorney
Joyce, Anderson & Meredith

**Mr. Greg Kern
Executive Director
Knoxville Community
Development Corporation

**Mr. Dwight Kessel
Knox County Executive

Mr. Rodney F. Lawler
President
Lawler-Wood Associates,
Incorporated

Mr. George A. Morgan
Chief Executive Officer and
Chairman of the Board
Valley Fidelity Bank and Trust
Company

- 252 -

**Mr. Jim Overbey
President
Downtown Knoxville
Association

*Mr. Robert J. Pennington
Attorney
Robert J. Pennington Law Office

*Mr. Richard E. Ray
Manager
Tennessee Operations
Aluminum Company of America
(ALCOA)

**The Honorable Jack Reagan
Mayor
City of Gatlinburg

*Mr. S. H. (Bo) Roberts, Jr.
President
Knoxville International Energy
Exposition, The 1982 World's
Fair

Mr. James H. Robinson
Director of Federal Programs
Knox City Schools

*Mr. Avon W. Rollins
Liaison Officer
Minority Economic
Development Staff
Tennessee Valley Authority

Mrs. Pat (Patsy) L. Scruggs
Civic Leader

**Mr. Don Sherwood
President
Blount County Chamber of
Commerce

*Mr. Thomas E. Sudman
*President and Chief Executive
Officer*
United American Service Corp.

Mr. Kyle C. Testerman
Attorney
Testerman, Hofferbert & Mills

****The Honorable Randy L.
Tyree**
Mayor
City of Knoxville

Mr. Al Underwood
President
Miller's, Inc

*Mr. Richard R. Van Sickle
President & Plant Manager
Rohm & Haas Tennessee,
Incorporated

Mr. H. Pat Wood
Vice President
Lawler-Wood Associates, Inc.

*Mr. Robert F. Worthington, Jr.
Attorney
Baker, Worthington, Crossley,
Stansberry & Woolf

*Mr. Lindsay Young
Attorney
McCampbell, Young, Bartlett,
Hollow & Marquis

THE 1982 WORLD'S FAIR
MAY 1 - OCTOBER 31

HIGHLIGHTS

May, 1982

May 1	President Ronald Reagan opens The 1982 World's Fair in Knoxville, Tennessee
May 2	Mary Travers - Tennessee State Amphitheatre
May 4	Glen Campbell and Jerry Lee Lewis - Tennessee State Amphitheatre
May 4-8	Rudolf Nureyev appears with the Boston Ballet in "Don Quixote"- Knoxville Civic Auditorium
May 6	The Stroh Brewery Company Special Day
May 6-8	The Aldridge Sisters - Tennessee State Amphitheatre
May 8	Avon Women's 10k Road Race - Downtown Knoxville
May 9	Tamburitzan Folk Ensemble - Auditorium
May 10-11	Richie Havens - Tennessee State Amphitheatre

May 10-14   "Ain't Misbehavin'" - Auditorium

May 12   Special session of the 92nd Tennessee General Assembly held in the Tennessee State Amphitheatre, marking the first time the legislature has convened in Knoxville since 1833

May 13-14   Riders in the Sky - Tennessee State Amphitheatre

May 16   One million visitors to date

Jim Turner with the Knoxville Symphony Orchestra - Tennessee State Amphitheatre

Robert Shaw in Concert with the Atlanta Symphony and Chorus – Auditorium

May 17-20   The "Bob Braun Show" is broadcast live from the Tennessee State Amphitheatre

May 17-23   Folk Medicine Week - Folklife Festival

May 18-20   Korean Court Music and Dance - Auditorium

May 19   Republic of Korea National Day

May 21   Stokely–Van Camp Special Day

May 21-22   Jimmie Walker - Tennessee State Amphitheatre

May 22	His Royal Highness Hassan bin Talal Crown Prince of the Hashemite Kingdom of Jordan, visits the World's Fair
May 23	Madame Imelda R. Marcos, First Lady of the Republic of the Philippines and Minister of Human Settlements, visits the World's Fair
	McLain Family Band - Tennessee State Amphitheatre
May 24-27	The third International Energy Symposium is held with Madame Marcos, U. S. Secretary of Energy James Edwards, and representatives of 33 nations participating. Dr. Armand Hammer, Chairman, Occidental Petroleum, serves as Chairman of the final session.
May 24	Scottish Athletic Events Exhibition - Court of Flags
May 24-30	Irish American week - Folklife Festival
May 25	Charlélie Couture - Tennessee State Amphitheatre
May 26	France National Day
May 28	North Carolina State Day
May 28-29	Steppe Brothers - Tennessee State Amphitheatre

May 29	Comedian Bob Hope celebrates his 79th birthday at the World's Fair during an appearance with Lynn Anderson at the Knoxville Civic Coliseum
May 30	Two million visitors to date
May 31	European Community National Day
	Jasmine – Tennessee State Amphitheatre

June, 1982

May 31-June 6	Furry Lewis Memorial Blues Week – Folklife Festival
June 2	Italy National Day
June 3	Peter Yarrow – Tennessee State Amphitheatre
	Royal Lipizzan Stallions – Coliseum
June 6	Chet Atkins with the Nashville Symphony - Tennessee State Amphitheatre
June 7	John Hartford -- Tennessee State Amphitheatre
June 7-13	Storytelling Week -- Tennessee State Amphitheatre

June 10	André-Michel Schub with the Knoxville Symphony Orchestra – Tennessee State Amphitheatre
June 11	Canadian Brass – Tennessee State Amphitheatre
	Team Murray World Cup of BMX – Bearden High School, Knoxville
June 12	Three million visitors to date
	Republic of the Philippines National Day
	Manhattan Rhythm Kings – Tennessee State Amphitheatre
June 13	Mac Frampton Trio with the Oak Ridge Symphony – Tennessee State Amphitheatre
June 14-20	Family Week – Folklife Festival
June 15	Australian "Night of Stars" featuring Air Supply, Peter Allen, Rolf Harris, Julie Anthony and Col Joye – Auditorium
June 16	Australian National Day
	The Kinks in Concert – Coliseum

June 17-19   The Ink Spots – Tennessee State Amphitheatre

June 18   Rolf Harris "Coojeebear and the Monster"
– Auditorium

June 18-20   The National Athletic Congress USA/Mobil Track &
Field Championships – UT Tom Black Track, Knoxville

June 20   Big Bird with Livonia Youth Symphony
– Tennessee State Amphitheatre

June 21-22   Ava Barber – Tennessee State Amphitheatre

June 23   United Kingdom National Day

Lover Boy in Concert – Coliseum

June 23-24   International Baseball Tournament
– Bill Meyer Stadium

June 24   Helen Cornelius – Tennessee State Amphitheatre

Jerry Lee Lewis in Concert with Johnny Rodriguez
– Coliseum

June 25   Four million visitors to date

June 25-26   Jennifer Muller/The Works
– Tennessee State Amphitheatre

June 26   "Up With People" Special Day

June 27   Occidental Petroleum Special Day
                 Peter Nero with the Knoxville Symphony Orchestra
                 – Tennessee State Amphitheatre

June 28   United States of America National Day

June 28-29   Jeff Lorber Fusion – Tennessee State Amphitheatre

July, 1982

July 1-3   Dave Loggins – Tennessee State Amphitheatre

July 4   The United States Pavilion and The 1982 World's
                 Fair present a Fourth of July "Star Spangled
                 Spectacular" with Johnny Cash; sell-out crowd of
                 46,000 in Neyland Stadium

                 Keith Brion as John Philip Sousa
                 – Tennessee Stadium Theatre

July 5   Arab Republic of Egypt National Day

July 5-11   Occupational Week - Folklife Festival

July 8   John Tate vs. Leroy Boone Boxing Match – Coliseum

July 9-10 USA Gymnastics

July 10 Y.M.C.A. Special Day

July 11 Roberta Peters with the Knoxville Symphony
Orchestra – Tennessee State Amphitheatre

July 12 Five million visitors to date

Japan National Day

July 12-17 Fantasy of Japan – Tennessee State Amphitheatre

July 13-18 The 1982 World's Fair presents the Grand Kabuki
Theatre of Japan, Knoxville Civic Auditorium; six
historic performances

July 15 Attendance surpasses the 5.2 million attendance
figure set at the Expo '74 in Spokane, Washington

Flav-O-Rich Special Day with Ray Stevens

Kamloops Rube Band
– Tennessee State Amphitheatre

July 16 Junior Olympics Torch Lighting Ceremony
– Court of Flags

Chicago in Concert – Coliseum

July 17-18   U.S.C.A. Kayak Marathon Invitational – Clinch River

World's Fair Invitational Rugby Tournament
– Forks of the River Park

July 18   TN Governor Lamar Alexander performs with the
Knoxville Symphony Orchestra – Tennessee State
Amphitheatre

July 19   The London Symphony in Concert – Auditorium

July 19-25   Radio Reunion Week
– Tennessee State Amphitheatre

July 20   Space Shuttle Astronauts Ken Mattingly and Henry
Hartsfield commemorate "NASA DAY" at the
World's Fair

Van Halen in Concert – Coliseum

July 21   Federal Republic of Germany National Day

The Stokely-Van Camp Folklife Festival presents the
"Knoxville Old Time Radio Reunion," a salute to the
heyday of radio in East Tennessee

July 22   Stokely-Van Camp Board of Directors Special Day

Ronnie Milsap and Brenda Lee in Concert – Coliseum

July 22-23.   Maxene Andrews -- Tennessee State Amphitheatre

July 24   Alaska State Day

                   Rick Springfield in Concert – Coliseum

July 25   Richard Trythall with the Oak Ridge Symphony
                   – Tennessee State Amphitheatre

July 26-27   Tracy Nelson – Tennessee State Amphitheatre

July 28   Six million visitors to date

                   Peru National Day

July 29   Dr. Arturo J. Borga, Peruvian archaeologist, directs
                   the ceremonial unwrapping of a 600-year-old
                   mummy at the Tennessee State Amphitheatre

July 30   Carlos Montoya – Tennessee State Amphitheatre

August, 1982

July 31-
Aug. 1   The Warsaw Philharmonic presents two standing-
                   room only concerts in the Tennessee State
                   Amphitheatre

Aug. 2	Gene Cotton – Tennessee State Amphitheatre
Aug. 2-8	Native American Week - Folklife Festival
Aug. 5	People's Republic of China National Day
Aug. 5-7	Jon Hendricks – Tennessee State Amphitheatre
	ABA-USA Basketball Tournament – Coliseum
Aug. 9	United Foods Special Day
	Rufus Thomas and Freedom Express Band – Tennessee State Amphitheatre
	Al Hirt and Pete Fountain in Concert – Coliseum
Aug. 10	The Chieftains – Tennessee State Amphitheatre
Aug. 12	Vacations of the Future Special Day
	REO Speedwagon in Concert – Coliseum
Aug. 13	"Chorus Line" – Auditorium
	James Taylor in Concert – Coliseum
Aug. 13-14	Five Blind Boys with the Staple Singers – Tennessee State Amphitheatre

Aug. 14   Seven million visitors to date

                 The Pittsburgh Steelers and the New England
                 Patriots attract 93,000 spectators to an NFL
                 Exhibition Game in Neyland Stadium

                 Carey/Bell Limousine Special Day

Aug. 15   Skitch Henderson with the Knoxville Symphony
                 Orchestra – Tennessee State Amphitheatre

Aug. 16   Salute to East Tennessee Mayors and Counties

                 Cathedralite Special Day

                 Willie Nelson in Concert – Coliseum

Aug. 16-18   National White Water Slalom Championships
                 – Ocoee River

Aug. 17   Hungarian People's Republic National Day

Aug. 18   István Lantos in Concert with the Knoxville
                 Symphony Orchestra – Auditorium

Aug. 19   Cheap Trick in Concert with Joan Jett – Coliseum

Aug. 20   Fairfield Communities Special Day
                 with John Newcombe

Aug. 21   Boy Scouts of America Special Day

Aug. 23   Canada National Day

Aug. 23-25   Canada Presents "Surprising Energy"
                       – Tennessee State Amphitheatre

Aug. 26   America's Electric Energy Exhibit Special Day

                       Loretta Lynn in Concert – Coliseum

Aug. 26-28   Pete Barbutti – Tennessee State Amphitheatre

                       U.S. National Swim Team vs. U.S.S.R. National Swim
                       Team – UT Aquatic Center

Aug. 27-29   National Slo-Pitch Softball Championships
                       – Bill Meyer Stadium

Aug. 30   Today's Solar Home Special Day

Aug. 30-31   Ricky Skaggs – Tennessee State Amphitheatre

September, 1982

Sept. 1   Knoxville College Special Day

Sept. 2   The 30,000[th] group tour bus arrives at the World's
                       Fair's North gate

                       Hartco Circus Special Day

Sept. 2-3	Papa John Creach – Tennessee State Amphitheatre
Sept. 3	Kingdom of Saudi Arabia National Day
Sept. 5	Eight million visitors to date
	Thousands of spectators give comedian Red Skelton a standing ovation in the Tennessee State Amphitheatre
Sept. 6	Labor Day Salute
Sept. 6-7	The Association – Tennessee State Amphitheatre
Sept. 6-12	Women's Culture Week – Folklife Festival
Sept. 7	Rotary International Special Day
	Leontyne Price in Concert – Auditorium
Sept. 8	Tennessee Valley Authority Special Day
Sept. 9-11	Ballets Jazz Montreal – Tennessee State Amphitheatre
Sept. 10-12	PGA Cup Matches – Holston Hills Country Club, Knoxville
Sept. 13-19	Coal Mining Week – Folklife Festival

Sept. 15   Grand Ole Opry Star Roy Acuff celebrates his 79th birthday in the Tennessee State Amphitheatre with 1,400 well-wishers

Sept. 18   Mexico National Day

Sept. 20   American Business Women's Special Day

Sept. 22   African-American Special Day

Leonard Rose and Issac Stern in Concert with the Knoxville Symphony Orchestra – Auditorium

Sept. 23-25   The Ventures – Tennessee State Amphitheatre

Sept. 24   His Excellency Ferdinand E. Marcos, President of the Republic of the Philippines and Madame Marcos, visit the World's Fair on the occasion of the State Visit to the United States

McKee Baking Company Special Day

Sept. 24   Merle Haggard with Razzy Bailey and Terri Gibbs – Coliseum

Sept. 26   Nine million visitors to date

South Carolina State Day

John Burstein as "Slim Goodbody" with the Middletown Youth Symphony – Tennessee State Amphitheatre

Sept. 28   Former U.S. Vice President Walter Mondale tours the World's Fair site

Sept. 29   Eastern Caribbean Special Day

Sept. 30   U.S. Marine Corps Special Day

October, 1982

Sept. 30-
Oct. 2   The Four Freshmen – Tennessee State Amphitheatre

Oct. 2   Spokane, Washington "Expo '74" Special Day

Oct. 3   Riverboat Ragtime Review
            – Tennessee State Amphitheatre

Oct. 4   Veterans Day Ceremony

Oct. 5   Gilman Paint Company Special Day

Oct. 7   United Way Special Day

Oct. 8   Fairfield Communities is selected as future developer of the Lower Second Creek Valley, site of The 1982 World's Fair

Indoor Soccer League Exhibition Game – Coliseum

Oct. 8-10   The Houston Ballet – Auditorium

Oct. 9   Former U.S. President Jimmy Carter and Mrs. Carter honored in a ceremony recognizing Carter's role in the development of the World's Fair

The World's Fair attracts a record single-day crowd of 102,842

Attendance reaches 9,630,000, surpassing the 9.6 million figure set at Seattle, Washington's "Century 21" Exposition, 1962

Khmer Dancers – Tennessee State Amphitheatre

Oct. 10   Peace Links Special Day

Conway Twitty in Concert – Coliseum

Oct. 11   Baptist Ministries Special Day

Oct. 11-12   Christy Lane – Tennessee State Amphitheatre

Oct. 11-17	Harvest Week – Folklife Festival
Oct. 14	Word Processing Services Special Day
Oct. 14-16	Leon Redbone – Tennessee State Amphitheatre
Oct. 15	Ten million visitors to date
	Oklahoma State Day
	Knoxville International Energy Exposition repays its $30 million bank loan
Oct. 17	Music and Dance of the Silk Route – Tennessee State Amphitheatre
Oct. 18	Parent – Teacher Association Special Day
Oct. 18-24	Family Week – Folklife Festival
Oct. 19	DuPont Special Day
Oct. 20	W. Stewart Evans, originator of the World's Fair idea, and 400 World's Fair ambassadors honored at Founder's Day ceremony, Tennessee State Amphitheatre
Oct. 21-23	Kinesis – Tennessee State Amphitheatre

Oct. 23	The Boston Celtics and the Philadelphia 76ers play an NBA Exhibition game before a sell-out crowd in Stokely Athletic Center
	Prague Symphony in Concert – Auditorium
Oct. 24	Seventh-day Adventist Church Special Day
Oct. 25	San Francisco Western Opera Theatre – Auditorium
Oct. 28-30	Kingston Trio – Tennessee State Amphitheatre
Oct. 29	The 16-member World's Fair Management Committee honored for service, dedication, and support in a special recognition ceremony
Oct. 30	The World's Fair exceeds the 11 million attendance projection set by Economics Research Associates, one day before closing
	Sir Alexander Gibson in Concert with the Scottish National Orchestra – Auditorium
Oct. 31	The 1982 World's Fair concludes with a final total attendance of 11,127,786 visitors

International Participants
(Listed in Order of Diplomatic Acceptance)

*In Residence

UNITED STATES OF AMERICA

*The Honorable Dortch Oldham
United States Commissioner General

The Honorable Joe M. Rodgers
Commissioner General of the United States Section

*Mr. Allen E. Beach
Deputy Commissioner General of the United States Section

ITALY

*His Excellency Alberto Balladelli
Commissioner General of the Italian Section

*Mr. Giuseppe Cipolloni
Deputy Commissioner General of the Italian Section

*Mr. Romolo Stazio
Secretary General of the Italian Section

FRANCE

The Honorable Hubert Cousin
Commissioner General of the French Section

*Mr. Alaine LeBel
Deputy Commissioner General of the French Section

FEDERAL REPUBLIC OF GERMANY

The Honorable Dr. Ernst Ingendaay
Consul General and Commissioner General of the Federal Republic of Germany

*Mr. Erich G. H. Urmoneit
Deputy Consul General and
Resident Commissioner General of
the Federal Republic of Germany
Section

*Mr. Anselm B. Jaenicke
Deputy Commissioner General of
the Federal Republic of Germany
Section

*Mrs. Ursula Jaenicke
Secretary General of the Federal
Republic of the Germany Section

THE UNITED KINGDOM

The Honorable Trevor Gatty
Her Britannic Majesty's Council
and Commissioner General of the
United Kingdom Section

*Mr. Ernest Lewis
Deputy Commissioner General of
the United Kingdom Section

*Mr. Dennis Dyer
Secretary General of the United
Kingdom Section

THE COMMISSION OF EUROPEAN COMMUNITIES

(Representing additionally:
Belgium, Denmark, Greece,
Ireland, Luxembourg and the
Netherlands)

The Honorable Franz Froschmaier
Commissioner General of the
European Community Section

*Mr. Andries Ekker
Deputy Commissioner General of
the European Community Section

JAPAN

The Honorable Ryo Kawade
Consul General and Commissioner
General of the Japanese Section
President of the Steering
Committee

Mr. Helichi Hamaoka
Deputy Commissioner General of
the Japanese Section

*Mr. Ippei Takeda
Secretary General of the Japanese Section

AUSTRALIA

*The Honorable Eric Wigley
Commissioner General of the Australian Section

*Mr. John Maddern
Deputy Commissioner General of the Australian Section

MEXICO

The Honorable Antonio Montes de Oca
Commissioner General of the Mexican Section

Mr. Alfonso Covarrubias
Deputy Commissioner General of the Mexican Section

*Mr. Anuar Karam
Resident Commissioner / Deputy Commissioner General of the Mexican Section

ROYAL KINGDOM OF SAUDI ARABIA

*The Honorable Ibrahim F. Khoja
Commissioner General of the Saudi Arabian Section

*Mr. Jean R. AbNader
Pavilion Director of the Saudi Arabian Section

REPUBLIC OF KOREA

The Honorable Dong Woon Chu
Consul General and Commissioner General of the Republic of Korea Section

*Mr. Hae-Soo Chung
Deputy Commissioner General and Director of the Republic of Korea Section

*Ho Taek Park
First Director of the Republic of Korea Section

CANADA

*The Honorable John M. Powles
*Commissioner General General of
the Canadian Section*

*Mr. Pierre Morin
*Deputy Commissioner General of
the Canadian Section*

HUNGARIAN PEOPLE'S REPUBLIC

The Honorable Dr. László Kapolyi
*State Secretary and Commissioner
General of the Hungarian People's
Republic Section*

*Mr. Antal Molnar
*Deputy Commissioner General of
the Hungarian People's Republic
Section*

PEOPLE'S REPUBLIC OF CHINA

*The Honorable Lu Feng Chun
*Commissioner General of the
People's Republic of China Section*

*Mr. Han Dexin
*Deputy Commissioner General
of the People's Republic of China
Section*

REPUBLIC OF THE PHILIPPINES

*The Honorable Joselito A. Castro
*Commissioner General of the
Republic of the Philippines Section*

*Mr. Francisco C. Duban
*Deputy Commissioner General
of the Republic of the Philippines
Section*

*Mr. Honorio J. Viray
*Deputy Commissioner General
of the Republic of the Philippines
Section*

*Mr. Teodoro C. Tiongson
*Secretary General and Pavilion
Director of the Republic of the
Philippines Section*

ARAB REPUBLIC OF EGYPT

The Honorable Yahia Kabil
Commissioner General of the Arab Republic of Egypt Section

*Mr. Joel Freedman
Director of the Arab Republic of Egypt Section

*Mrs. Lou Potter
Pavilion Manager

PERU

*The Honorable Jorge Boza, Jr.
Commissioner General of the Peruvian Section

*Mr. Jose Boza
Director of the Peruvian Section

Corporate Participants

African-American Exhibit

Alaska Seafood Marketing Institute

ALCOA/Reynolds Metals

American Express Company

American Gas Association/Gas Exhibits, Inc.

American Hardware Supply Company

American Home Foods

America's Electric Energy Exhibit, Inc.

Amliner American Coaches, Inc.

Anheuser-Busch, Inc.

Ashland Oil

Avis Rent-A-Car Systems, Inc.

Avon

Baptist Ministries

Bunn-O-Matic Corporation

Carey of Knoxville/Bell Limousine

Cathedralite Dome Homes

The Laurel Church of Christ

The Church's Presence

Cimarron Carpets, Inc.

The Coca-Cola Company

COMSAT

Conergy Marketing, Inc

Control Data Corporation

Council of Energy Resource Tribes

Dairymen, Inc.

Delta Air Lines

E. I. DuPont de Nemours

Eastern Caribbean Tourist Association

Eastman Kodak Company

Entertainment Computer Sales, Inc.

Expo Pro Shop, Inc.

Fairfield Communities

Federal Express Corporation

Ford Motor Company

Gatlinburg Chamber of Chamber of Commerce

General Electric

Gerber Products Co.

Gilman Company, Inc.

Greyhound Lines, Inc.

H. J. Heinz Company

Hosea International

IBM Corporation

Ice Brokers, Inc.

JFG Coffee Company

Kern's Bakery, Inc

Kimball Piano and Organ Company, International, Inc.

Kingtron Corporation

Knoxville Health Pavilion/City of Knoxville

Lay Packing Company

Leaf & Tree Company

McKee Baking Company

Miller Brewing Company

The Murray Ohio Manufacturing Company

Myrtle Beach Grand Strand/South Carolina National Travel, Inc.

Niagara Therapy Manufacturing Corp.

North American Phillips/Magnavox

Occidental-Petroleum

Park National Bank

Phillips Business Systems

Phillips Information Systems

Professional Puppets, Inc.

Remington Rand Corporation

Schering-Plough Corporation

Seventh-day Adventist Church

Shopsmith

Shriner's

South Central Bell

Stokely-Van Camp, Inc.

Stroh Brewery Company

Sun Company

Tennessee Valley Authority

Tenneco, Inc

Texaco

Tibbals Flooring Company

Terminix

U. S. Steel-Oilwell Division

Union Carbide Corporation

United American Bank

United American Solar Group

United Foods

United States National Park Service

The United States Postal Service

Vacations of the Future

Video Expo, Inc.

Wyndham Investment Corp.

Word Processing Services

Yale Security Division/Scovill

Participating States

Georgia
Kentucky
North Carolina
Oklahoma
South Carolina
Tennessee
West Virginia

Technological Innovations & Two Other Fun Items

*Introduction of the first "Resistive Touchscreen Technology," aka "AccuTouch," forerunner of today's smartphone screens, created by prolific inventor Dr. G. Samuel Hurst of the Oak Ridge National Laboratory, who earned his doctorate at UT-Knoxville

*First Pay-at-the-Pump" technology was demonstrated by Texaco

*Cherry Coke—The clear winner among the flavors test-marketed at the World's Fair

*Tetra Pak Ultra Heat Treatment (UHT) no refrigeration milk, introduced by Dairymen, Inc.

*Bell Telephone demonstration of the world's first mobile phone

*Most Popular Novelty Item—Deely Boppers: More than 2 million of the plastic headbands with two antennae holding sparkly spheres on the top were sold at the World's Fair

*Among the Most Popular Food Items: Petro's featured chili poured over a bag of Fritos with topping options of sour cream, chopped onions, diced tomatoes, shredded cheddar and jack cheese, black olives and chopped jalapeños

Statistics at a Glance

Special Category International Exposition, sanctioned by the Bureau of International Expositions, Paris, France
Theme: "Energy Turns the World"
184 Days, May 1-October 31,1982
23 nations from six continents participated
91 corporate participants
Seven state participants
Ticket prices: $9.95 (Ages 12-54) $8.25 ((Children under 11)
$9.25 (Adults over 55)
Total Attendance: 11,127,786 visitors
Slogan: "You've Got to Be There!"
Iconic Structures/Buildings: 266-foot-tall Sunsphere, the Tennessee State Amphitheatre, the U.S. Pavilion, the Steohaus, the L&N Station, the 10-foot-tall, 1200 pound Rubik's Cube, which stood outside of the Hungarian People's Republic pavilion, and the Candy Factory

THE 1982 WORLD'S FAIR MANAGEMENT STAFF

PRESIDENT & CHIEF EXECUTIVE OFFICER
S. H. (Bo) Roberts, Jr.

EXECUTIVE CONSULTANT
King F. Cole

EXECUTIVE VICE PRESIDENT
James E. Drinnon, Jr.

EXECUTIVE OFFICES
Jon B. Brock - Assistant to the President
Cookie Crowson - Assistant to the President
Richard Jacobs - Assistant to the President
Bill Newton - Director, Project Control
Jack Rankin - Executive Staff Coordinator
Sharon Wells - Administrative Assistant

COMMUNICATIONS
C. William Carroll - Vice President
Leigh R. Hendry - Director
Joey Popp - Director
Jim Friedrich - Manager
Denise McKenzie - Assistant Manager
Susannah Holben - Senior Editor
Marion Kozar - Administrative Assistant
Marynell Ward - Administrative Assistant

CONTRACT MANAGEMENT
George M. Siler - Executive Vice President
Jimmy Lou Wright - Director
Doug Ebbs - Manager

ECONOMIC DEVELOPMENT
Theotis Robinson - Vice President
Paul Middlebrooks
Venice Peek

ENERGY PROGRAMS
Walter N. Lambert - Executive Vice President
Nelda M. Kersey - Assistant Vice President
W. Stewart Evans - Director, Special Projects
Nan Lintz
Kathy Murphy
Julia Walker - Gold Passport Coordinator

FINANCE
C. K. Swan, III - Executive Vice President
Randy Miller - Controller
Cindy Auble - Director, Revenue Accounting
Pat Hutsell - Director, Expenditure Accounting
Harry Michaels - Director, Concessions Accounting
Terry Hasson - Box Office Manager
Diane Rutherford - Purchasing Manager
Barbara Ragland - Executive Assistant
Diane Irwin - Administrative Assistant

LEGAL

H. Peter Claussen - Vice President

Ken Cutshaw - Attorney

William Booker - Attorney

LIBRARY

Jane Row - Librarian

Nancy Underwood - Assistant Librarian

MARKETING

William R. Francisco - Executive Vice President

Julian Forrester - Vice President, World Festival

Sandra Bowers - Director of Administration, World Festival

Fred Lounsberry - Director, Admission Sales

Rich Sibley - Director, Creative Services

Dick Van Kleeck – Director, Folklife Festival

Michael Blachly - Director, Special and National Days, World Festival

Lotta Gradin-Dick - Director, Special and National Days, World Festival

Bill Schmidt - Director, Sports, World Festival

Gloria Richardson - Manager, Budget / Contracts, World Festival

Scott Tillery - Event Manager, World Festival

Warren Clark - Music Services Manager, World Festival

Anetha Shipe - Performing Arts Manager, World Festival

Jim Thorpe - Senior Artist, Creative Services

Judy Holdredge - Performing Arts Assistant Manager, World Festival

Tom Crowder - Assistant, World Festival

PERSONNEL

Ed Litrenta - Director

Deby Roberson - Personnel Management Specialist

Nancy Crider - Personnel Training Coordinator

SITE DEVELOPMENT/OPERATIONS

Edward S. Keen - Executive Vice President

L. James Benedick - Vice President, Operations

Charles D. Smith - Vice President, Site Development

Alice Buckley - Director, Budget Control, Operations

Ed Cureton - Director, Emergency Medical Services

Buck Mathias - Director, Food and Beverage Concessions

John Whitney - Director, General Services

Dave Sirianna - Director, Merchandise Concessions

Fred Rankin - Director, Physical Facilities

Bill Fox - Director, Security/Emergency Medical Services

Pete Soukup - Director, Support Services

John Bruner – Director, Transportation Services

Lance Tacke - Director, VIP Services

John Underwood - Assistant Director, Security

Gary Nichols - Manager, Food and Beverage Concessions

Paul Pearson - Manager, Food and Beverage Concessions

Terri Lanza - Manager, Merchandise Concessions

Carroll Logan - Manager, Pavilions

Cathy Higdon - Special Events Manager

Chuck Miller - Support Services Manager

Gordon Scott - Support Services Manager

Betty Miller - VIP Services Manager

James Hamrick - Security Supervisor

Ken Lett - Key Control

MAY 1982

S	MAY 1	87,659
S	MAY 2	40,001
M	MAY 3	57,300
T	MAY 4	48,690
W	MAY 5	53,370
R	MAY 6	44,107
F	MAY 7	56,671
S	MAY 8	85,709
S	MAY 9	55,748
M	MAY 10	61,314
T	MAY 11	71,286
W	MAY 12	66,038
R	MAY 13	61,740
F	MAY 14	90,224
S	MAY 15	99,306
S	MAY 16	58,547
M	MAY 17	76,600
T	MAY 18	82,029
W	MAY 19	72,952
R	MAY 20	64,381
F	MAY 21	92,892
S	MAY 22	96,223
S	MAY 23	60,781
M	MAY 24	75,845
T	MAY 25	78,822
W	MAY 26	65,967
R	MAY 27	57,210
F	MAY 28	67,510
S	MAY 29	96,080
S	MAY 30	75,472
M	MAY 31	49,991

JUNE 1982

T	JUNE 1	65,325
W	JUNE 2	73,360
R	JUNE 3	63,768
F	JUNE 4	61,916
S	JUNE 5	80,394
S	JUNE 6	62,276
M	JUNE 7	83,501
T	JUNE 8	88,657
W	JUNE 9	71,819
R	JUNE 10	66,076
F	JUNE 11	74,851
S	JUNE 12	77,872
S	JUNE 13	69,130
M	JUNE 14	94,594
T	JUNE 15	97,019
W	JUNE 16	73,090
R	JUNE 17	73,946
F	JUNE 18	75,476
S	JUNE 19	81,033
S	JUNE 20	64,107
M	JUNE 21	88,499
T	JUNE 22	93,531
W	JUNE 23	79,736
R	JUNE 24	68,875
F	JUNE 25	67,074
S	JUNE 26	72,480
S	JUNE 27	62,273
M	JUNE 28	76,498
T	JUNE 29	80,630
W	JUNE 30	65,197

GRAND TOTAL TO DATE FOR MAY: 2,150,465

GRAND TOTAL TO DATE FOR JUNE: 4,403,346

JULY 1982

R	JULY 1	54,750
F	JULY 2	48,362
S	JULY 3	51,818
S	JULY 4	67,479
M	JULY 5	55,386
T	JULY 6	67,032
W	JULY 7	69,590
R	JULY 8	61,596
F	JULY 9	54,793
S	JULY 10	60,088
S	JULY 11	53,531
M	JULY 12	68,233
T	JULY 13	71,556
W	JULY 14	63,907
R	JULY 15	56,282
F	JULY 16	52,599
S	JULY 17	54,789
S	JULY 18	51,999
M	JULY 19	61,717
T	JULY 20	70,265
W	JULY 21	59,035
R	JULY 22	48,724
F	JULY 23	51,986
S	JULY 24	52,685
S	JULY 25	50,021
M	JULY 26	59,733
T	JULY 27	66,812
W	JULY 28	58,452
R	JULY 29	52,710
F	JULY 30	50,819
S	JULY 31	45,292

**GRAND TOTAL TO DATE
FOR JULY: 6,195,509**

AUGUST 1982

S	AUG 1	54,213
M	AUG 2	63,148
T	AUG 3	71,358
W	AUG 4	59,815
R	AUG 5	54,274
F	AUG 6	53,975
S	AUG 7	54,817
S	AUG 8	52,869
M	AUG 9	57,421
T	AUG 10	74,213
W	AUG 11	59,521
R	AUG 12	35,309
F	AUG 13	54,857
S	AUG 14	63,442
S	AUG 15	56,685
M	AUG 16	57,105
T	AUG 17	58,682
W	AUG 18	51,453
R	AUG 19	47,831
F	AUG 20	46,772
S	AUG 21	55,041
S	AUG 22	45,013
M	AUG 23	40,513
T	AUG 24	44,212
W	AUG 25	40,748
R	AUG 26	41,756
F	AUG 27	40,967
S	AUG 28	49,679
S	AUG 29	41,501
M	AUG 30	31,997
T	AUG 31	31,090

**GRAND TOTAL TO DATE
FOR AUGUST: 7,805,786**

SEPTEMBER 1982

W	SEPT 1	24,029
R	SEPT 2	23,014
F	SEPT 3	33,130
S	SEPT 4	55,929
S	SEPT 5	78,089
M	SEPT 6	42,744
T	SEPT 7	33,869
W	SEPT 8	38,918
R	SEPT 9	37,969
F	SEPT 10	43,395
S	SEPT 11	59,707
S	SEPT 12	44,962
M	SEPT 13	45,820
T	SEPT 14	46,293
W	SEPT 15	46,288
R	SEPT 16	41,219
F	SEPT 17	47,934
S	SEPT 18	72,464
S	SEPT 19	51,522
M	SEPT 20	41,120
T	SEPT 21	47,011
W	SEPT 22	51,121
R	SEPT 23	40,239
F	SEPT 24	46,492
S	SEPT 25	60,760
S	SEPT 26	48,954
M	SEPT 27	37,549
T	SEPT 28	43,818
W	SEPT 29	39,182
R	SEPT 30	38,465

**GRAND TOTAL TO DATE
FOR SEPTEMBER: 9,167,792**

OCTOBER 1982

F	OCT 1	51,984
S	OCT 2	86,193
S	OCT 3	67,993
M	OCT 4	45,611
T	OCT 5	47,088
W	OCT 6	43,400
R	OCT 7	36,344
F	OCT 8	53,695
S	OCT 9	102,842
S	OCT 10	74,594
M	OCT 11	51,961
T	OCT 12	47,019
W	OCT 13	35,955
R	OCT 14	55,196
F	OCT 15	69,005
S	OCT 16	95,217
S	OCT 17	73,238
M	OCT 18	52,366
T	OCT 19	55,556
W	OCT 20	46,185
R	OCT 21	51,787
F	OCT 22	65,255
S	OCT 23	96,745
S	OCT 24	80,699
M.	OCT 25	45,220
T	OCT 26	53,040
W	OCT 27	60,254
R	OCT 28	70,423
F	OCT 29	78,770
S	OCT 30	80,689
S	OCT 31	85,670

**GRAND TOTAL TO DATE
FOR OCTOBER: 11,127,786**

The 1982 World's Fair ATTENDANCE FIGURES

Monthly Attendance Figures

MAY   2,150,465
JUNE   2,253,003
JULY   1,792,041
AUGUST   1,610,277
SEPTEMBER   1,362,006
OCTOBER   1,959,994

TOTAL 11,127,786

Highest Attendance
Saturday, October 9   102,842

Lowest Attendance
Thursday, September 2   23,014

Average Attendance   60,477 / Per Day

THE 1982 WORLD'S FAIR DESIGN TEAM

EXECUTIVE ARCHITECTS/ENGINEERS AND PLANNERS
A Joint Venture

McCarty Bullock Holsaple, Inc., Architects
Bruce McCarty, FAIA, Executive Architect/Planner
Charles D. Smith, AIA, Design Coordinator 1976 - 1980
Douglas McCarty, AIA, Design Coordinator 1980 - 1982

Barge Waggoner Sumner and Cannon, Engineers
William H. Cannon, P. E., Executive Engineer
Don Mauldin, P. E., Project Engineer

CONSULTANTS
R. Duell & Associates, Inc. - Site Planning
Barton Aschman Associates, Inc. - Transportation & Parking Planning
Famco Engineering, Inc. - Structural Engineering
Geologic Associates - Soils Engineering
I. C. Thomasson - Mechanical & Electrical Engineering
handprints/Atelier 105 – Environmental Graphics Design
Levitan Design Associates, Inc. - Exhibit Design
Pageantry World, Inc. - Pageantry
Rucker & Associates - Specialty Lighting

ASSOCIATED ARCHITECTS
Adams Craft Herz and Walker - Entrance Gates and Service Buildings
Barber & McMurry - Renovated Buildings
Community Tectonics - International Pavilions
Dewitt S. Dykes - Merchandising and Snack Shops
Eugene Burr - Renovated Houses & Folklife
Lindsay and Maples - International Pavilions
McDuffie and Associates - Merchandising and Snack Shops
McKissack and McKissack - Renovated Building

CONSTRUCTION MANAGER
Rentenbach Engineering Company

Honors & Non-Profit Service

S.H. (Bo) Roberts, Jr.

Recipient of the **Ernie Pyle Memorial Award** at the University of Tennessee-Knoxville; named for American journalist and Pulitzer Prize-winning WWII war correspondent; presented to the most outstanding senior journalism graduate by the UT School of Journalism

Recipient of the **Sigma Delta Chi Award**, at the University of Tennessee- Knoxville; presented to the most outstanding senior journalism graduate, by the UT-K Society of Professional Journalists chapter

Recipient of the **Edward J. Meeman Foundation Award** for Editorial Writing; named for noted Tennessee newspaper editor and Pulitzer Prize nominee; presented in consecutive years for excellence in editorial writing, Memphis, TN

Past Member, **Kappa Tau Alpha** at the University of Tennessee-Knoxville; college honor society recognizing excellence and scholarship in journalism and mass communications

Honoree, Outstanding Young Man, **Tennessee Jaycees**, Nashville, TN

Honoree, Salesman of the Year, **Knoxville Sales and Marketing Executives**, Knoxville, TN

Past Member and Director, **Sevierville Rotary Club**, Sevierville, TN

Past Member and Board Secretary, **Sevierville Jaycees**, Sevierville, TN

Past President and Fund Chairman, **American Cancer Society**, Sevier County chapter, Sevierville TN

Founding Board Member and Past Vice President, **Sevierville Chamber of Commerce**, Sevierville TN

Past Member, **Tennessee Press Association,** statewide trade organization for newspapers, Knoxville, TN

Past Member, **Sevier County Court Industrial Commission**, Sevierville, TN

Past Vice President, **UT Alumni Association**, Sevier County chapter, Sevierville, TN

Past Member, **Dogwood Arts Festival Committee**, Knoxville, TN

Past Chairman, **United Way of Knoxville,** Knoxville, TN

Past Vice Chairman, **1976 Tennessee American Revolution Bicentennial Commission,** Nashville, TN

Past Member, **Metropolitan Planning Commission,** Knoxville, TN

Past Member, Board of Directors, **YMCA,** Knoxville, TN

Past Member, **Greater Knoxville Chamber of Commerce**, Knoxville, TN

Past Member, **American Cancer Society**, DeKalb County chapter, Atlanta, GA

Past Designated Member by TN Governor Buford Ellington, **National Governors' Conference, Committee on State-Urban Relations,** Chicago, ILL

Past Member, **Tennessee Commission on Inter-governmental Affairs,** Nashville, TN

Past Member, Advisory Board, **Travel South USA,** Atlanta, GA

Past Member, **Board of Control, Tennessee Law Enforcement Training Academy,** Nashville, TN

Past Member, **Advisory Committee, Tennessee Industrial Research Service,** Nashville, TN

Past Co-Chairman, **Appalachian Regional Commission,** Washington, D.C.

Past Member, **Democratic Platform Committee Staff,** Washington, D.C.

Past Chairman, **TN State Fair Commission,** Nashville, TN

Past Chairman, Fundraising Committee, **Statue Committee Honoring Tennessee State University Track Coach Ed Temple,** Nashville, TN

Past Board of Directors Member, **Nashville Wine Auction, l'Ete du Vin**, benefitting the American Cancer Society, Nashville, TN

Board Member, **Nashville Sports Council**, Nashville, TN

Member, **Alumni Legislative Council**, University of Tennessee

* * *

*Consultant to **The Music City Bowl, the Tennessee Road Builders Association Foundation, Tennessee Tech University, and former consultant to Tennessee State University and the Tennessee Board of Regents**

ADDENDUM II

Early Years
Akron, Ohio and Oak Ridge & Harriman, Tennessee

It was the first day of spring when Samuel Herbert Roberts, Jr. came on to the scene. My mother told me that it was snowing that day (March 21st), which was not that unusual in Akron, Ohio. Two days later, the first major decision in my life occurred when my father, who had me anointed me as a "Junior," suddenly became concerned that I would be called "Junior." He promptly nicknamed me "Bo" (obviously, without consulting me). At the time, he greatly admired Indiana University's football coach, Bo McMillin. The name became prophetic, given my love of football and almost every other sport on the athletic spectrum.

Despite having been born there, I don't have strong memories about Ohio. We lived in what seemed to be a nice house, in a neighborhood where the homes surrounded a small lake where kids could ice skate in the winter. I recall my brother being born when I was three, and that we had a dog, a Scottish terrier named, "Butch," who preceded me into the family. Entering the first grade in Akron, one of my most vivid memories was discovering—while my parents were still present—this phenomenon that if you stuck your leg out that someone would trip.

And, when they tripped, it caused much laughter among the other children. None of the other parents thought it was very funny, though, and certainly my parents didn't. I got straightened out pretty quickly, however; whether it was by my mother, the teacher, or both of them together, I learned a new lesson in record time.

My father had been working in Akron with the Firestone Tire and Rubber Company. He was there because there weren't many jobs in the recession-plagued South. He needed a job. He left Harriman, Tennessee, to visit his older sister, Gladys and her husband, Roy West. Dad got a job, and later met Roy's sister, Vera, who had traveled from her Georgia home for a visit. To make a long story short, a couple of years later, the families became further intertwined when Roy's sister married Gladys's brother. Vera Mabel West became a Roberts, which is the genesis of how we got to Akron in the first place. We left there not long after I finished the first grade.

There was a major construction project underway in East Tennessee, in a little place called Oak Ridge. Both Dad and Uncle Roy received offers for positions there; both accepted, and off we trekked to the Volunteer State. Oak Ridge was in the midst of a multitude of transitional activities. It was a Federal city, established virtually in the middle of nowhere, near the newly created power system of dams operated by the Tennessee Valley Authority (TVA). Our first home was a flat top structure, hastily built, on a foundation of wood stilts, but accommodating enough. Most streets in Oak Ridge were still primarily mud. But, with construction everywhere, it was an exciting place for a kid. We initially lived on Jersey Lane, before moving up in the world to Dewey Road, into a house that was built on a foundation, in a ranch-military style, a design shared by all the residences in the neighborhood.

Oak Ridge was actually a terrific experience, as it was completely fenced-in, and, therefore, considered secure. Anyone coming or going had to pass through a security checkpoint and present official credentials. The public transportation system was vital, as few residents had cars, and, for those who did, the rationed gasoline was precious. We enjoyed some of the first"shopping centers" in the country, so it was quite common for me, as a seven-or-eight-year-old, to hop on a bus unchaperoned, go to the hobby store and then catch a bus back home. This made an early impression on me about the value of public infrastructure. I think I still yearn for it, wondering why we abandoned trolley cars? The other great thing was that softball was introduced to the South in Oak Ridge during that time, and I watched many spirited games there.

Then some momentous news emerged that two atomic bombs had been detonated over the Japanese cities of Hiroshima and Nagasaki. It was then revealed that these nuclear weapons were a result of a gigantic, top-secret undertaking, called "the Manhattan Project." Oak Ridge played a significant role in the development of the Project. Oddly, these bombings were cause for people to come out of their houses and start celebrating. Some knew what they were doing in Oak Ridge, but I'm surmising that a large number of employees in the city had no idea what they were making. In any event, it was a time of celebration and I remember adults dancing in the streets. There were also billboards that read, "Loose lips sink ships." Maintaining that secrecy was impressive, even if, as a kid, I didn't know why the hell they were being so secretive. After the second bomb was dropped three days after the first, World War II was soon concluded. Another wild celebration took place. Anti-Japanese headlines, which would now be considered highly politically incorrect, appeared in such respected newspapers as the *Knoxville News-Sentinel*. There were big fireworks displays and Oak Ridgers all seemed deliriously happy with the outcome and proud to have contributed.

A couple of additional notes about Oak Ridge: My father's family is from East Tennessee. Their original home was in a community called Wheat, Tennessee, which happened to be in the center of what became Oak Ridge. My grandfather was a contractor serving Roane and Anderson counties. His company built Robertsville School not far from Wheat, which became Robertsville Junior High School, and still stands today in Oak Ridge. I'm proud to say that it has been preserved as an historic building. The Roberts family graveyard is nearby.

Interestingly, I never got to attend my namesake's junior high school. By then, I was in the fifth grade, because after I finished the second grade, my teachers met with my parents and said I needed to go straight to the fourth grade, as I was "not being challenged" enough. This was another decision made for me about which I was not consulted. However, to this day, I use it as a valid excuse for the poor quality of my penmanship, as third grade was the year where one learned that thing called "cursive writing" ...which, I am told, is no longer legally required in U.S. schools.

Sometime during the middle of the fifth grade, just after the war, my father decided to join his cousin in a family business about 20 miles away from Oak Ridge in Harriman, where he grew up, and where my grandfather had been prosperous as a contractor prior to the Great Depression. It sits in a valley that abuts the edge of the Cumberland Mountains to the west, and is a bumpy, 35-mile drive to Knoxville, in the foothills of the Great Smoky Mountains, to the east.

My father later showed me their beautiful white house on a hilltop where he grew up; unfortunately, it didn't survive the Depression. Harriman was founded in the late 19th century as a "beacon of sobriety," and was planned as a community for those who would not tolerate either the demon rum or other spirits. The Baptist church was dominant, and people did not drink—in public, at least. That lasted a few years, before it evolved into a typical, small Southern town, complete with a large paper mill and a couple of substantial textile mills. The population count was about 10,000 when I lived there, and remains so today.

My first day in school was in a church because the Harriman elementary and junior high schools had burned. The different grades were scattered throughout local churches. The fifth grade was in the Methodist church, where I had an interesting first day of school. Mother took me there to enroll. I was the first new kid on the block in quite a while—not to mention that I was the kid who still spoke like a Yankee, which was anything that sounded different from the typical East Tennessee twang—an accent which is more pronounced than either of those in middle or west Tennessee.

During recess that morning, I had about 15 or 20 rather anxious young men come up to me and suggest that we meet after school to fight. I guessed that was their standard "ritual of welcome," but that wasn't the way they phrased it, of course. Each of them came to me individually and wanted to take me on, fist to fist, after school. I sort of reluctantly agreed, while thinking I was going to spend a long time after school getting to know these boys. As I walked the two blocks home for lunch, I was mulling things over, thinking, well, this may not be the best way to spend an early evening after school. The more I thought about it, the more it seemed as though my stomach was beginning to ache.

Meanwhile, several of the teachers learned about the plethora of challenges looming in front of me and called my mother. They conferred, resulting in those boys receiving a serious chewing out. Fortunately, I didn't get beat up. We worked things out because none of the various threats transpired. At the time, I thought we had a healthy mix of students in our school. There were some who looked a lot like me who lived in the city, and then there were those from the farms, as well as others who had rougher edges, regardless of where they lived. While we had an interesting group, we were all white, of course (but more about that later).

As things moved along, I remember seventh grade classes were held in the Baptist church; the mix of students was beginning to change a bit. There were guys, and a few girls, who were quite a bit older, and were basically in a holding pattern, waiting to reach the age of 17, when they would no longer be required to attend school. What I learned academically in seventh grade, I'm not certain; I learned much more about life, primarily the trials and travails of puberty. I had become popular with the female students, which I ascribed to my Yankee accent. On Saturdays, I would go to the movies. While Hopalong Cassidy, Gene

Autry, and Roy Rogers galloped across the screen, I practiced kissing with different girls in five-minute sessions. They would pointedly let me know if some girls, unfairly, received more kissing time than the others.

Thinking back, life was pretty good. We were in the post-war period with a healthy economy; most people were feeling upbeat. For me, summers were primarily relegated to playing baseball and being lazy. While my family wasn't wealthy, my brother and I never wanted for anything, as we were quite comfortable.

I played football in high school, as a fairly average player. Later, I became the place kicker, and in my first game in that position, kicked the extra points to beat Lenoir City (a huge rival) for the first time in 12 years. This was the moment where I tasted a touch of fame within a very small circle. It felt dang good. Then an injured leg restricted me to a kick after the first touchdown. We would fake it and I would pass for the point after subsequent scores. My career record in passing for the mighty Blue Devils was 11 for 11, a record never to be broken (because stats on extra point passes were not recorded, I can still make this dubious claim).

During the next couple of years at school, some of us guys got a little rowdy when we could. Actually it started during our sophomore year. Though I was the youngest, I looked like the oldest because I was shaving early. I became the designated beer-buyer. While our search for alcohol was relentless, it was only occasionally successful (hard cider was a real treat). Just as it went with the girls we were attracted to, we talked like we did much more than anything that actually happened.

When I look back on my young driving experiences, I see that time as the most ridiculous of my entire life. We would do such dangerous things as "playing chicken" on curves, passing other cars. Somehow, and only by the grace of God, did we manage to survive that time period unscathed. My parents' 1948 Nash sure got banged up, though.

My attendance pattern at school became a lot more irregular when I discovered that school carried right on without me, whether I showed up or not. I often had to scramble toward the end of the year to make sure that I had logged enough days to get promoted to the next level. I had never been involved in school politics, but during my senior year we had a legendary, extremely strict teacher, named Ms. Clarisse Bunch. She was an icon in the community, and had taught my father, along with the parents of most of the other students in our class. An English teacher, she was also the senior class sponsor, and an instructor who was a ball of fire, but in a very, very proper way. She was honored on several occasions prior to her retirement years later, and I was humbled to give the keynote address at her community-wide recognition celebration. Anyway, some of the girls and guys got together and went to Ms. Bunch and said they wanted to talk me into running for president of the senior class. She gave her approval. I thought they must all be crazy, but I was duly elected, much to my surprise. Toward the end of the school year, I recall Ms. Bunch sitting at her desk, tapping her foot impatiently, saying, "Well, I see the president of our class decided to join us today." She was annoyed with my irregular attendance, but I suppose I did alright, as I was still selected to speak at graduation.

I don't remember exactly what I said, but I'm sure it was filled with platitudes and was all about the future. I did ask Ms. Bunch to check my grammar in advance. Her impeccable reputation as a superior taskmaster was so widely known, that teachers at the University of Tennessee (UT) knew that you'd know proper English if you'd attended Harriman High. Even though I wasn't the most attentive student, Ms. Bunch recognized potential. In my speech, I reflected on how one person like Ms. Bunch could influence and change one's life for the better.

I was by no means an exemplary student but did alright if I was either admonished by a teacher or happened to take a particular liking to a subject. Math was one of those that I enjoyed. Before I even knew what algebra was, I'd been using multiplication and division to figure out batting averages and other sports stats.

There was a new-to-town male history teacher who'd moved to Harriman and wanted to become "one of the guys," especially with some of us football players and supposed "school leaders." He would buy beer for us, and joke around with us; we took unbelievable advantage of that in his classroom, where we did little work, goofed off and still received A grades. The principal must've been made aware of this situation, because later that year, we started receiving D's or worse. My friends selected me to lead a private protest to the teacher regarding our grade changes. I borrowed a switchblade knife from one of my rougher friends, which I took into the history classroom. I flipped it over and over, sticking it into my wooden desktop. I told the teacher that if our grades didn't change that day, he was to meet me at 6 p.m. that night in front of Shivers' family restaurant where we were going to have it out. Of course, I had no intention of using a knife; I was just trying to reinforce my toughness, which was a complete façade. Six o'clock came and went while we waited and waited and waited.

The teacher never showed up. At school the next day, we saw that the teacher's office had been cleared out, and he was gone. We were never told exactly what had happened, but we could guess. Some of the students were saying that I had run him off. I neither declined credit nor took the blame.

The good news and the bad news was that grades now had to be earned during what was left of that school year. A young lady came in to replace the teacher who'd departed. She was tough, but fair. She was very encouraging, and in just three months, she'd ignited my love affair with history. Reading and learning about the history of the world, and the history of our country, became my new passion. I loathe the circumstances which led to my discovering this new love for learning, as things could've easily turned disastrous. I probably got much more than I deserved. Fortunately, I retained my interest in history, but abandoned the use of switchblades and false bravado.

Another kind of life-changing event occurred early during my senior year that opened my eyes to the reality of race in the South. The principal called two or three of us into his office and said that the school needed more patrol boys to assist with the safety of students and traffic in the mornings. He wanted the football players to take on this task, so I became captain of the safety patrol. We were issued our belts, which we proudly wore, while taking the duty seriously, and making it fun. We recruited, did marching drills, and, though we tried not to show it, took pride in what we were doing. It also meant arriving at school earlier than normal. While I stood there as the mist was rising in the mornings, I saw the yellow school buses filled with Black students coming from Oliver Springs (25 miles away) to the Black county high school in Rockwood. I would stare at those kids as they passed by and they would stare right back at me, sheer curiosity emanating from both sides. I would often think: "Why does this make sense? Why are we doing this? Why do they have to be separate?" That's when I began thinking about how it felt to be different.

During the summer, I had gotten to know some African-Americans because we lived near the town's baseball park. I played baseball all the time then and would join the practices of the town's Black team. This was the first time that I had ever interacted with people of color. My mother and father were both good, church-going people, but they grew up in the South with prejudices that pre-dated them by several generations (not making excuses here, just painting an accurate picture about how things really were then.) It was a place where the N-word was used with frequency; not necessarily in a derogatory manner, but just as a general reference point. I recall that so clearly throughout my childhood. If either my brother or myself picked up something from the ground, and put it in our mouths, our parents were quick to say: "Get that out of your mouth; an N-word might've had that in their mouth!" And, man, it was just like saying: "Wipe that off right now! It might be dirty or don't do that because it might have serious germs on it." These statements were made as casually as saying "bless you!" when someone sneezed. They weren't being intentionally cruel, but the words were certainly cruel.

Several years later, when I was long past the age of putting unsanitary things in my mouth, that phrase really began to wear on me. During my junior or senior year, I talked to my mom and dad and asked them not to use the N-word again in my presence. They respected that request, and I never heard them say it again. I was not a crusader, but I felt strongly that it was wrong to treat human beings as "less than." I intentionally involved myself with people of color. I learned that while we had different pigmentation, the baseballs were all the same color: as in dirty from bouncing on the ground. My beliefs would later draw the ire of the KKK early in my journalism career.

Another important life lesson I learned was that of humility. As time passed, I found plenty of reasons to be humble. During my junior year, our English teacher selected four of us to perform in a one-act play. It was a drama, not a comedy, about a prisoner condemned to death. I had the role of a newspaper reporter. Freshly enchanted by this new "craft," we worked quite hard and presented the play several times for the other students. We also presented it in the evening so that parents were able to attend. Our teacher felt that we were good enough to be entered in the regional competition, held on the Tennessee Tech University campus in nearby Cookeville. To our immense delight, we actually won, and I received the outstanding actor award. Though shocked by our victory, I have to admit that it felt great to return home having taken the top prize at the regionals. We were now ready to take on the entire state at the finals at the University of Tennessee in Knoxville. We (and I) were certainly feeling cocky about our chances. We performed as well as we had in Cookeville, but we didn't scratch. Neither our play, nor my performance, received any special accolades when the awards were announced. Any visions we might have harbored about wowing Hollywood in the future were immediately dashed. We all discovered that humble pie wasn't a very tasty dish; but, it was another meaningful lesson.

Blessed as I was with a deep, nicely modulated voice, and by virtue of being friends with the Mayor's son (the family which owned the local radio station), I had an inside track at an opportunity to become a part-time disc jockey at night. The station was very tame, very controlled and very white-oriented; its listenership was a mirror image of itself. "Black music" was not permitted on this station at that time. However, most kids our age would surreptitiously get in their cars at night to pick up the clear channel radio station, WLAC in Gallatin, Tennessee. We were all avid listeners of *Randy's Record Hi-Lights,* a showcase of the day for the emergence of "Black music." Bill "Hoss/ Hossman" Allen was the prime DJ during those late evenings and a key player in the worldwide dissemination of that musical genre. Decades later, one of the thrills of my life was having lunch with Hoss and my friend, Elizabeth McDonnell Yoder (now Fox), the general manager of WLAC in Nashville. I told Allen he had shaped the lives of thousands of teenagers in the Southeast with his dissemination of "Black music." During my time as a young turk DJ at our local station, I quickly saw that the pay levels were not particularly remunerative, and whenever I would slip in a slightly Black piece of music, the Mayor would immediately call to say "get that off the air now!" I think that adequately conveys the tenor of the race situation in the mid-1950s in Harriman.

U.S. *Air Force*

Several weeks in advance of graduation, I saw a promotional film about the U.S. Air Force. It inspired me and offered a path forward to achieving my short-term goals. My plan was to join the Air Force soon after graduation, have some excitement, learn a little, and be eligible to go to college on the G.I. Bill. I was so enamored with this idea that I also talked my friend and classmate, Curtis Jones, into joining me on this grand adventure. We committed and 30 days after our high school graduation, we were on a train bound for San Antonio, Texas to begin our military service. It took three days to get there. We arrived on July 5th and found that San Antonio was the hottest place we'd ever been (but it was a "dry heat," as the saying goes). Due to the holiday weekend, we were not issued uniforms until three days following our arrival, so still in our original traveling clothes, made for a rather odiferous start to our Air Force careers.

We proceeded through basic training, which most military people will recall, is not the most pleasant experience, as it's a time of being torn down. One learns how low in life one is, before being built back up and told that one is not so bad after all, as long as the concept of taking orders is crystal clear. Seven or eight weeks into basic training, Curtis came to me, said he hated me, that I had ruined his life, and that he hoped to never see me again. He could not fathom how I had persuaded him to join the Air Force. He stuck it out, though, remaining in the Air Force for 24 years, before he retired. We later became friends again.

If the temperature reached 95 degrees, drills would be halted. Of course, when it hovered around 93 or 94 degrees, we prayed like hell for temperatures shown on the parade field thermometer to edge past 95. I developed blisters on my feet from all the marching and then someone stepped on my foot in a movie theatre, the blisters burst and became infected. I ended up in the hospital for six days, my only hospitalization during the first 70 years of my life. When I was released, I had to switch to a training unit that was a week behind my original group.

After completing basic training in San Antonio in September (after three grueling months of summer heat), my first assignment was at

Parks Air Force Base in Pleasanton, California. I took my first air-plane ride to San Francisco and went across the bay to Parks (which no longer exists, as it was phased out decades ago), near Hayward, California. It was an interesting time to be assigned to duty at Parks as it was the processing center for all outgoing and incoming soldiers with duty in the Pacific. There weren't many outgoing, but there were droves of soldiers incoming because the Korean War was then nearing its end. Despite being virtually over, I still qualified for the G.I. Bill, because I had enlisted just in time. Thousands of troops were return-ing daily, and being processed, with some assigned duties at Parks. The result was that we had approximately three airmen for every work position, creating a sporadic work schedule. It was a lot like being on a temporary vacation. During my first leave, which was to get married, I talked a fellow airman (and my first Black friend in life, Watsey Lum-barger) into working one shift for me, which allowed me to leave 10 days before my leave officially started.

I didn't make much money at the rank of airman third class, but I lived on base, had three daily meals free and had free housing, so I was able to do a little traveling in San Francisco, where I fell in love with the Bay Area. It was an eye-opening time for me. The city itself captured my heart and imagination like no other place I had ever been. I attend-ed my first National Football League game at Kezar Stadium. With the SF 49ers hosting the Chicago Bears, I saw the unbelievable running back, Hugh McElhenny play, along with the Bears' fantastic rookie re-ceiver, Harlon Hill. The Bears won 31-27, a stupendous game which ignited my lifelong love of the NFL.

I also received my first gambling lesson while in San Francisco. Right after payday, my friends would entice me to join them at the Golden

State racetrack. I knew absolutely nothing about horse racing, except that the fastest horse ostensibly won. I was not at all informed about the dangers of betting, so I refrained from participating much. That was a wise approach, as I came to find out, after seeing some of my friends lose their entire paychecks. I also noticed that the people in the grandstand area were not as well-dressed as those in the box seats, who were sporting fur coats and fashionably cut suits. Their approach to betting also seemed to be far less stressful. I quickly realized that to make money gambling, one needed to be in a position to afford to lose. This was yet another valuable life lesson.

There were many more to come.

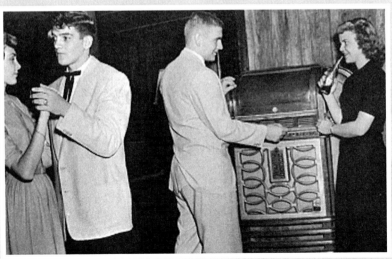

Me and my sons, circa 1983. L-R Andy, Sam, me, Mark. *Photo courtesy Rip Noel*

Leigh R. Hendry, Editor
Photo courtesy Jerry Atnip